A Peacemaking Approach to Criminology

A Collection of Writings

Louis J. Gesualdi

University Press of America,® Inc.
Lanham • Boulder • New York • Toronto • Plymouth, UK

Copyright © 2014 by University Press of America,® Inc.
4501 Forbes Boulevard, Suite 200, Lanham, Maryland 20706
UPA Aquisitions Department (301) 459-3366

10 Thornbury Road, Plymouth PL6 7PP, United Kingdom

Library of Congress Control Number: 2013946893
ISBN: 978-0-7618-6214-7 (paper : alk. paper)—ISBN: 978-0-7618-6215-4 (electronic)

∞™ The paper used in this publication meets the minimum requirements of American
National Standard for Information Sciences Permanence of Paper for Printed Library
Materials, ANSI/NISO Z39.48-1992.

This book is dedicated to my friend and colleague
Professor H. Craig Collins

Contents

Preface

A peacemaking approach to criminology is a humanistic perspective to criminology. It is a humane, nonviolent and scientific approach in its treatment of crime and the offender. A peacemaking approach to criminology deals with prevention of crime and rehabilitation of offenders, and involves principles of social justice and human rights. The collection of writings chosen for this book demonstrates a peacemaking approach to criminology.

Chapters 1 and 2 present the case for a different way about dealing with crime known as a peacemaking approach to criminology (which includes restorative justice).

In chapters 3 and 4, research points out the miscarriages of justice in the United States involving capital punishment and discrimination in the administration of the death penalty.

Chapter 5 presents data that show the restricted options that poor youth have as a result of a small amount of economic chances alongside a lack of concerned adults.

In chapters 6 and 7, research demonstrates that socioeconomic conditions create and maintain cultural values associated with racial and ethnic inequality (poverty) and that these values are not the primary factors in explaining behavioral characteristics.

Chapter 8 presents data that refute the claim that the black single-female-headed household is a major cause of America's high crime rates.

In chapter 9, research indicates that affirmative action is not the cause of a failing meritocracy in America.

Chapter 10 shows how different crime related problems and issues have been twisted into myths.

In chapter 11, the economic and political aspects of white-collar deviance are discussed.

Chapter 12 places the source of the United States' crime rates in the values and behavior of American society.

In chapters 13 and 14, the harmful acts committed by the well-off are analyzed.

Chapter 15 demonstrates the severe damage many people experience as an outcome of fraudulent small group health insurance businesses.

In chapters 16 and 17, the harmful acts committed by elites are examined.

Chapter 18 provides data that demonstrate the unethical behavior and harmful acts of expanding corporations moving their factories and plants into Third World countries.

In chapter 19, the successful work of John Augustus in probation exemplifies the principles of peacemaking criminology.

Chapters 20 and 21 demonstrate that retributive justice does not reduce the rate of crime among teenagers and adults.

In chapter 22, the initial stages of a plan for a development of economic democracy are presented.

It is this author's wish that these 22 chapters will stimulate a desire by the reader to become interested in peacemaking criminology.

Acknowledgments

I make the following acknowledgements. A part of chapter one, "What Is A Peacemaking Perspective to Criminology?," was originally published by © Springer Science and Business Media B.V. as "John R. Fuller's *Criminal Justice: A Peacemaking Perspective*," in the journal *Crime, Law and Social Change*, Vol. 29, Number 1, January 1998, pp. 84-85, Louis Gesualdi, the author, with kind permission from Springer Science + Business Media B.V., and the other part of chapter one, "What Is A Peacemaking Perspective to Criminology?," was originally published by the Pi Gamma Mu, International Honor Society in Social Science as "A Review of Michael Braswell, John Fuller and Bo Lozoff's book *Corrections, Peacemaking and Restorative Justice: Transforming Individuals and Institutions*" in the journal *International Social Science Review*, 2001, Volume 76, Numbers 3 & 4, Louis Gesualdi, the author. The second chapter, "*Restoring Justice:* A Discussion," was originally published by Sage Publication as "Van Ness and Heetderks Strong's *Restoring Justice*," in the *Journal of Contemporary Criminal Justice*, August 1999, Louis Gesualdi, the author. Chapter 3, "A Look at *The Color of Justice*," was originally published by © Springer Science and Business Media B.V. as "Walker, Spohn and Delone's *The Color of Justice*," in the journal *Crime, Law and Social Change*, Vol. 28, No. 4, 1997, pp. 183-184, Louis Gesualdi, the author, with kind permission from Springer Science + Business Media B.V. The fourth chapter, "Bohm's *Deathquest*: A Brief Aspect," was originally published by © Springer Science and Business Media B.V. as "Bohm's *Deathquest: An Introduction to the Theory of Capital Punishment in the United States*" in the journal *Crime, Law and Social Change*, Volume 31, Number 2, March 1999, pp. 154-155, Louis Gesualdi, the author, with kind permission from Springer Science + Business Media B.V. Chapter 5, "Youth Living in Poverty," was originally published by the American Soci-

ological Association as "Williams and Kornblum's *Growing Up Poor*: A
Review" in the journal *Teaching Sociology,* Vol. 16, Number 2, April 1988,
Louis Gesualdi, the author. The sixth chapter, "Steinberg's *Ethnic Myth*: An
Explanation," was originally published by Western Washington University
as "Steinberg's *Ethnic Myth: Race, Ethnicity and Class*" in *The Journal of
Ethnic Studies,* Volume 11, Number 4, 1984, Louis Gesualdi, the author.
Chapter seven, "A Review of Steinberg's *Turning Back,*" was originally
published as "Steinberg's *Turning Back*: A Review" in the magazine *The
Humanist,* Vol. 57, No. 4, 1997, Louis Gesualdi, the author. The eighth
chapter, "The Black Single Female Headed Family and Crime," was originally published as "Don't Blame Mom for Crime" in the magazine *The Humanist,* May/June 1998, Louis Gesualdi, the author. Chapter nine, "Popular Notions of Affirmative Action: A Criticism," was originally published by the
Pennsylvania Sociological Society as "Popular Notions of Affirmative Action: A Criticism" in the journal *Sociological Viewpoints,* Fall 2001, Louis
Gesualdi, the author. A part of chapter ten, "Kappeler, Blumberg and Potter's
The Mythology of Crime and Criminal Justice: A Brief Discussion," was
originally published by Sage Publications as "Kappeler, Blumberg and Pot-
ter's *The Mythology of Crime and Criminal Justice, 2 nd Edition:* A Review"
in the *Journal of Contemporary Criminal Justice,* Vol. 13, No. 4, 1997,
Louis Gesualdi, the author, and the other part of chapter ten, "Kappeler,
Blumberg and Potter's *The Mythology of Crime and Criminal Justice*: A
Brief Discussion," was originally published by Pi Gamma Mu as "Kappeler,
Blumberg and Potter's *The Mythology of Crime and Criminal Justice, 3 rd
Edition:* A Review" in the journal *International Social Science Review,*
Vol.75, Numbers 3 & 4, 2000, Louis Gesualdi, the author. The eleventh
chapter, "A Look into Simon and Hagan's *White-Collar Deviance,*" was
originally published by Sage Publications as "Simon and Hagan's *White-
Collar Deviance:* A Review" in the *Journal of Contemporary Criminal Jus-
tice,* Vol. 16, Number 4, November 2000, Louis Gesualdi, the author. Chap-
ter twelve, "A Brief Examination of Messner and Rosenfeld's *Crime and the
American Dream,*" was originally published by © Springer Science and
Business as "Messner and Rosenfeld's *Crime and the American Dream*: A
Review" in the journal *Crime, Law and Social Change 26,* Issue 1, March
1996, pp.96-97, Louis Gesualdi, the author, with kind permission from
Springer Sciences + Business Media B.V. The thirteenth chapter, "Reiman's
The Rich Get Richer and the Poor Get Prison: A Review," was originally
published by © Springer Science and Business Media B.V. as "Reiman's *The
Rich Get Richer and the Poor Get Prison*" in the journal *Crime, Law and
Social Change,* Volume 31, Number 2, March 1999, pp. 152-153, Louis
Gesualdi, the author, with kind permission from Springer Science + Business
Media B.V. Chapter 14, "Rosoff, Pontell and Tillman's *Profit without Hon-
or:* A Brief Analysis," was originally published by © Springer Science and

Business Media B.V. as "Rosoff, Pontell and Tillman's *Profit without Honor: White-Collar Crime and Looting in America*" in the journal *Crime, Law and Social Change,* Volume 29, Number 4, May 1998, pp. 354-357, Louis Gesualdi, the author, with kind permission from Springer Science + Business Media B.V. The fifteenth chapter, "Tillman's *Broken Promises*: A Brief Examination," was originally published by © Springer Science and Business Media B.V. as "Tillman's *Broken Promises:* A Review," in *Crime, Law and Social Change,* Volume, 31, Number 2, March 1999, pp. 151-152, Louis Gesualdi, the author, with kind permission from Springer Science + Business Media B.V. Chapter sixteen "An Examination of Simon's *Elite Deviance,*" was originally published by Sage Publications as "Simon's *Elite Deviance*: A Review" in the *Journal of Contemporary Criminal Justice,* Vol. 18, No. 1, February, 2002, Louis Gesualdi, the author. The seventeenth chapter, "A Review of Coleman's *The Criminal Elite,*" was originally published by the Pennsylvania Sociological Society as "Coleman's *The Criminal Elite: Understanding White-Collar Crime:* A Review" in the journal *Sociological Viewpoints,* Vol. 16, Fall 2000, Louis Gesualdi, the author. Chapter nineteen, "The Work of John Augustus: Peacemaking Criminology," was originally published by the Academy of Criminal Justice Science as "The Work of John Augustus: Peacemaking Criminology" in the newsletter *Academy of Criminal Justice Science ACJS Today*, Volume XVII, Issue 3, September/October, 1999, Louis Gesualdi, the author. The twentieth chapter, "The Popular Notion about Teenage Violence," was originally published by the Pennsylvania Sociological Society as "Males' *The Scapegoat Generation: America ' s War on Adolescents*: A Review" in the journal *Sociological Viewpoints,* Vol. 15, 1999, Louis Gesualdi, the author. Chapter twenty-one, "Peacemaking Acts and Programs to Cut Adult and Teen Crime," was originally published by the Pennsylvania Sociological Society as "Peacemaking Acts and Programs to Cut Adult and Teen Crime" in the journal *Sociological Viewpoints,* Vol. 19, 2003, Louis Gesualdi, the author. Second, I wish to thank Tom Ward, Associate Professor, College of Professional Studies, St. John's University, for our many conversations and discussions on criminology. Third, I would like to indicate my gratitude to Melissa King for formatting and editing my book. Finally, I wish to thank Lisa Kuan, my fiancée, for her enthusiasm and support for this book.

Introduction

A peacemaking approach to criminology is a humane, nonviolent and scientific approach in its treatment of crime and the offender. It looks at crime as just one of the many types of suffering that exemplify human life. Efforts to put a stop to such suffering, according to peacemaking criminologists, should take account of a main rebuilding of America's social institutions, such as the economic system and the criminal justice system, so that they no longer make suffering. Unemployment and incarceration are, respectively, characteristics of America's economic system and criminal justice system that require changes. In short, the U. S. as a society pays no notice to prevention but rather sticks to the belief of imprisonment and punishment. A peacemaking approach to criminology deals with prevention of crime and rehabilitation of offenders, and involves principles of social justice and human rights.[1] The collection of writings (twenty of the twenty-two were previously published) chosen for this book demonstrates a peacemaking approach to criminology.

Chapter one, "What Is A Peacemaking Perspective to Criminology?," discusses a peacemaking approach to criminology. It reviews John R. Fuller's book *Criminal Justice: A Peacemaking Perspective* and Michael Braswell, John Fuller and Bo Lozoff's work, *Corrections, Peacemaking and Restorative Justice: Transforming Individuals and Institutions.*

The second chapter, "*Restoring Justice:* A Discussion," makes suggestions for policy and practice for America's criminal justice system to balance the interests and needs of victims, communities, offenders and government. It asserts that the criminal justice system in the United States is in need of restorative justice.

Chapter three, "A Look at *The Color of Justice,*" indicates that the American criminal justice system is still characterized by racial and ethnic discrimination against minorities in certain situations or contexts.

The fourth chapter, "Bohm's *Deathquest*: A Brief Aspect," points out the miscarriages of justice in the United States involving capital punishment and discrimination in the administration of the death penalty.

Chapter five, "Youth Living in Poverty," points out the limited choices that poor youth have as an outcome of few economic opportunities along with a lack of caring adults.

The sixth chapter, "Steinberg's *Ethnic Myth*: An Examination," argues that traits attributed to one's cultural group need to be related to the larger social and economic conditions in which they are implanted. It points out that traits, which are often considered "ethnic" or "racial," may well be more directly related to class, locality and other socio-economic circumstances.

Chapter seven, "A Review of Steinberg's *Turning Back*," shows how mainstream social science,with the exception of the 1960s, failed to confront racism and champion civil rights. It indicates that many social scientists were not and are not willing to place responsibility for America's racial problems on political and economic institutions.

The eighth chapter, "Don't Blame Mom for Crime," is a reply to Daniel P. Moynihan and James Q. Wilson. It presents data that refute Moynihan and Wilson's assessment of what causes crime.

Chapter nine, "Popular Notions of Affirmative Action: A Criticism," presents data that do not support the notion that a magnificent meritocracy is not succeeding in the United States because of affirmative action.

The tenth chapter, "Kappeler, Blumberg and Potter's *The Mythology of Crime and Criminal Justice*: A Brief Discussion," questions the many widespread beliefs of deviance, crime and criminal justice in the United States. It examines and debunks many public myths regarding crime and criminal justice.

Chapter eleven, "David R. Simon and Frank E. Hagan's *White-Collar Deviance*: A Brief Discussion," discusses the economic and political aspects of white-collar deviance. It proposes changes in America's social and economic system in order to properly deal with white-collar deviance.

The twelfth chapter, "A Brief Examination of Messner and Rosenfeld's *Crime and the American Dream*," places the cause of the United States' crime rates in the values and behavior of American society. It asserts that high levels of crime in America (especially compared to other Western nations) are created from cultural and social situations that exist in the U.S.

Chapter thirteen, "Reiman's *The Rich Get Richer and the Poor Get Prison*: A Review," examines the harmful acts committed by the well-off. It points out the bias against the poor that exists within America's criminal justice system.

The fourteenth chapter, "Rosoff, Pontell and Tillman's *Profit without Honor*: A Brief Analysis," challenges the popular notion that white-collar crime is not dangerous. It points out that certain white-collar crimes cause environmental damage, personal injury, sickness and death.

Chapter fifteen, "Tillman's *Broken Promises*: A Brief Examination," uncovers the white collar crimes (scams) that occur in the small group health insurance industry. It makes known the serious harm many people have experienced as a result of fraudulent small group health insurance businesses.

The sixteenth chapter, "An Examination of Simon's *Elite Deviance,*" looks at the harmful acts committed by elites (i.e., members of the upper and upper-middle classes). It indicates that the source of elite deviance is the socio-economic structure of society.

Chapter seventeen, "A Review of Coleman's *The Criminal Elite,*" challenges the popular notion that white-collar crime causes less damage to the American public than street crime. It presents the 1996 National White-Collar Crime Center Conference's definition of white-collar crime and points out the types and causes of white-collar crime.

The eighteenth chapter, "Exploitation of Third World Labor," points out that a peacemaking approach to criminology examines unethical behavior and harmful acts occurring in Third World countries committed by corporations. Specifically, it discusses two studies that demonstrate such unethical behavior and harmful acts of these corporations.

Chapter nineteen, "The Work of John Augustus: Peacemaking Criminology," demonstrates that John Augustus' work in probation was quite successful and exemplified the principles of peacemaking criminology (involves not an authoritarian but a humane, nonviolent and scientific approach in its treatment of crime and the offender). This chapter argues that the implementation of alternative sanctions and a full employment bill is a continuation and expansion of John Augustus' successful work and would be supported by peacemaking criminology.

The twentieth chapter, "The Popular Notion about Teenage Violence," challenges the popular notion that America's teenagers are naturally violent. It points out that violent crime among youth is founded in social conditions such as poverty and income disparity and not age demographics and race.

Chapter twenty-one, "Peacemaking Acts and Programs to Cut Adult and Teen Crime," indicates that a peacemaking approach to criminology not only supports the implementation of different intermediate sanctions but also of changes in the social and economic structures of American society. These changes include a full employment bill, a real minimum wage, nationalized health care and ending the prohibition of drugs. The chapter asserts that such political acts and programs would provide adult and teen offenders rehabilitation and a real chance to better their lives.

The twenty-second chapter, "A Development of Economic Democracy," is the beginning of a blueprint for a development of economic democracy as discussed by Daniel DeLeon. This chapter argues that an economic democratic system may eliminate or significantly lower the amount of social problems associated with the market economy (such as unemployment, underemployment, poverty, unsafe work conditions, unsafe products and destruction of the environment).

The twenty-two writings are an introduction to an understanding of a peacemaking approach to criminology. It is the author's wish that this publication will stimulate a desire by the reader to become more interested in this humane approach to criminology.

NOTE

1. John R. Fuller, *Criminal Justice: A Peacemaking Perspective* (Boston: Allyn and Bacon, 1998) and Michael Braswell, John Fuller, Bo Lozoff, *Corrections, Peacemaking and Restorative Justice: Transforming Individuals and Institutions* (Cincinnati, OH: Anderson Publishing Company, 2001).

Chapter One

What Is a Peacemaking Perspective to Criminology?[1]

A peacemaking perspective to criminology, according to H. Pepinsky and R. Quinney[2], is a humanistic approach to criminology. This approach views crime as just one of the many forms of suffering (such as war, poverty, unemployment and others) that characterize human existence. It is involved with the advancement of humane, non violent, non authoritarian and scientific ways to reduce (and eventually end) suffering and oppression. A peacemaking viewpoint proposes major changes of the social and economic structures in the United States (as well as the rest of the world) so that these structures no longer bring about suffering and oppression.[3] This chapter examines John R. Fuller's book *Criminal Justice: A Peacemaking Perspective* and Michael Braswell, John Fuller and Bo Lozoff's book, *Corrections, Peacemaking and Restorative Justice: Transforming Individuals and Institutions,* to further comprehend the peacemaking viewpoint.

John R. Fuller's *Criminal Justice: A Peacemaking Perspective* gives a peacemaking viewpoint to criminal justice. It states that a peacemaking approach "emphasizes social justice, conflict resolution, rehabilitation and a belief that people need to cooperate in democratic institutions in order to develop meaningful communities."[4] The author's text states that this approach in its treatment of crime and the offender "looks both at the individual's culpability and at the contribution of the institutions of society."[5] Fuller's study presents a peacemaking perspective to such criminal justice issues as drug use, capital punishment, gun control and violence. His work demonstrates that this perspective is a humane, nonviolent and scientific way to effectively cut crime in America.[6]

Criminal Justice indicates that a peacemaking position to criminal justice supports drug decriminalization. The book declares that American society needs to view drug use as more of a public health problem than a criminal justice issue and suggests that there are benefits from drug decriminalization. First, the text explains that repealing drug laws will save billions of dollars a year in law enforcement. Second, the study makes apparent that organized crime would experience a severe setback as an outcome of drug decriminal-ization. Third, the work contends that the quality of life for many drug users would improve greatly if legal controls were removed.[7] For instance, many drug users may seek help without the fear of being arrested.

John R. Fuller points out that a peacemaking viewpoint to criminal justice rejects capital punishment on the grounds of social justice. He notes that factors such as social status and race "make it more likely that some will be executed while others who are equally guilty will be spared."[8] Moreover, the author makes evident that capital punishment is not an effective deterrent to murder.

Criminal Justice asserts that the accessibility of firearms is an important factor influencing the high rate of lethal violence in America. Fuller's book explains that "other countries have a much lower rate of lethal violence that can be attributed to the lack of availability of guns."[9] His work contends that from a peacemaking perspective more gun control laws need to be developed and enforced in order to reduce such violence in our nation.

John R. Fuller states that "poverty of our knowledge about violence and its prevention is considerable."[10] The author points out that a peacemaking perspective to violence advances the following suggestions. First, more fund-ing is needed for "programs and research efforts that might be able to iden-tify and prevent violent behavior."[11] Second, myths and stereotypes about violent offenders and their victims need to be exposed. Third, methodologi-cal issues in data collection and analysis of violent offenders need to be improved. Fourth, more rehabilitative programs need to be set up for violent offenders.[12]

Fuller's work *Criminal Justice: A Peacemaking Perspective* argues that a peacemaking perspective to criminal justice is highly successful in its treat-ment of crime and the offender.

Michael Braswell, John Fuller and Bo Lozoff's, *Corrections, Peacemak-ing and Restorative Justice: Transforming Individuals and Institutions,* gives a peacemaking perspective to criminal justice and society in general. Their work demonstrates that a peacemaking approach involves the use of humane, nonviolent and scientific ways to effectively deal with unethical behavior. Their book indicates that America's criminal justice system, through a peace-making viewpoint, can balance the needs of victims, communities, and of-fenders.[13]

Braswell, Fuller and Lozoff point out that a peacemaking viewpoint draws from a variety of ancient wisdom and religious traditions including Judaism, Christianity, Islam, Hinduism, Buddhism, Taoism and Native

American. In other words, the peacemaking perspective support and promote the tenets of peace and love (found in all religious traditions) in dealing with unethical behavior (for instance, peaceful movements for change by Gandhi and Martin Luther King). They also show how a peacemaking approach draws inspiration from feminism and critical criminology (see chapter "Exploitation of Third World Labor" as an example).[14]

Corrections, Peacemaking and Restorative Justice indicates how a peacemaking perspective is directly relevant to corrections. The book points out that a peacemaking approach is against capital punishment and the construction of super maximum-security prisons. It shows how capital punishment and super maximum-security prisons work against the reduction of violence in society. Moreover, the text argues that a peacemaking view sees rehabilitation programs for offenders as a way to protect society.[15]

Braswell, Fuller and Lozoff's *Corrections, Peacemaking and Restorative Justice* notes that restorative justice programs (such as victim-offender reconciliation programs, family group conferencing and victim offender panels) exemplify a peacemaking viewpoint. Their work points out that these programs allow victims and offenders to meet one another outside the courtroom to hold offenders culpable for their misdeeds and to have offenders make reparation to their victims. The text maintains that restorative justice programs can be of benefit to both victim and offender and that the criminal justice system in the United States is in need of these programs.[16]

Overall, Braswell, Fuller and Lozoff argue that a peacemaking perspective can be highly successful in dealing with unethical and criminal behavior. The authors point out that an individual can develop a peacemaking approach to criminal justice and society and become a force for personal and social peace[17] (see chapter "The Work of John Augustus: Peacemaking Criminology" as an example).

NOTES

1. Parts of this chapter were originally published as Louis Gesualdi, "John R. Fuller's *Criminal Justice: A Peacemaking Perspective,*" *Crime, Law and Social Change* 29, no. 1 (1998): 84, and as Louis Gesualdi, "A Review of Michael Braswell, John Fuller and Bo Lozoff's book *Corrections, Peacemaking and Restorative Justice: Transforming Individuals and Institutions,*" *International Social Science Review* 76, no. 3 & 4 (2001): 141.
2. Harold Pepinsky and Richard Quinney, eds., *Criminology as Peacemaking* (Bloomington: Indiana University Press, 1991).
3. Ibid.
4. John R. Fuller, *Criminal Justice: A Peacemaking Perspective* (Boston: Allyn and Bacon, 1998), 41.
5. Ibid., 43.
6. Fuller, *Criminal Justice: A Peacemaking Perspective.*
7. Ibid.
8. Ibid., 231.
9. Ibid., 197.

10. Ibid., 170.
11. Ibid., 179.
12. Fuller, *Criminal Justice: A Peacemaking Perspective.*
13. Michael Braswell, John Fuller, and Bo Lozoff, *Corrections, Peacemaking and Restorative Justice: Transforming Individuals and Institutions* (Cincinnati, OH: Anderson Publishing Company, 2001).
14. Ibid.
15. Ibid.
16. Ibid.
17. Ibid.

Chapter Two

Restoring Justice

A Discussion[1]

Daniel Van Ness and Karen Heetderks Strong's *Restoring Justice* successfully presents the case for a different way of thinking about crime known as restorative justice (a part of peacemaking criminology). Restorative justice

> focuses on repairing the harm caused by crime and reducing the likelihood of future harm. It requires offenders to take responsibility for their actions and for harm they have caused. It seeks redress for victims, recompense by offenders and reintegration of both within the community. It is achieved through a cooperative effort by communities and the government.[2]

Restoring Justice makes suggestions for policy and practice for America's criminal justice system to balance the interests and needs of victims, communities, offenders, and government. The book asserts that the criminal justice system in the United States is in need of restorative justice.[3]

Van Ness and Strong point out that criminal justice in America, unlike Western European countries, is based on retributive justice. Retributive justice views crime as an act against the government, as a violation of law, and as an individual act with solely individual responsibility. It leaves the dilemma of crime to the government alone, and it assigns major roles of the criminal justice system only to the government and the offender. In a criminal justice system based on retributive justice, it is believed that punishment deters crime and changes behavior. Furthermore, retributive justice weighs success by how much punishment has been given to the offender. The authors make evident that retributive justice based on the high rates of violence and crimes in the United States (past and present) has had very little to no success.[4]

9

The restorative justice model views crime as an act against a person or community. Restorative justice acknowledges that offenders harm victims, communities and even themselves. Crime, according to restorative justice, has both individual and social dimensions of responsibility. Van Ness and Strong's work makes clear that punishment alone is not effective in changing behavior, and it is disruptive to community harmony and good relationships. The authors note that in a criminal justice system based on restorative justice, victims are central to the process of resolving a crime, and offenders need to make reparation. Moreover, restorative justice gauges success by how much harm has been mended or hindered. The authors convincingly argue that a criminal justice system based on restorative justice can succeed. [5]

Van Ness and Strong maintain that justice is best served when victims, offenders and communities receive equitable attention in the criminal justice process. They indicate that although offenders need to take responsibility for their acts, the responsibility for restoring mutual respect, understanding and support among those involved must be shared by the community and the government. The authors suggest several ways in which victims, offenders, communities and the government can be involved in America's criminal justice system. Crime victims, for example, will receive restitution or other reparation from the offender. Crime victims will be encouraged to give input at all points in the criminal justice system as to how the offender will rectify the harm. They will have the chance to face the offenders and tell their stories. When needed, crime victims will receive support, assistance, reimbursement, information and services from the community and government. Offenders will compensate their victims and will render meaningful service to pay back their debts to their communities. They will face the personal harm caused to their victims by participating in restorative justice programs (victim awareness programs). [6]

Offenders will receive work experience and complete tasks that increase skills and improve the community. They will be supervised to the greatest extent possible by the community. In addition, offenders will gain decision-making skills and be given opportunities to help others. Community and government entities will be involved in rehabilitation, community safety initiatives, and holding offenders accountable. They will work with offenders on community service projects, and they will provide aid to offenders as mentors, employers and supporters. Efforts will be undertaken in both the private and public sectors to set up work opportunities for offenders so that they may earn the money necessary to pay restitution to victims. In addition, service opportunities that allow offenders to make important contributions to the improvement of community life will be available. The community will advise courts and corrections, and the community will play a major role in the sentencing process. [7]

Overall, Van Ness and Strong show that victims and offenders are generally more satisfied when they have participated in a criminal justice system based on restorative justice than in a system based on retributive justice.[8]

Restoring Justice describes three restorative justice programs (victim-offender reconciliation programs, family group conferencing, and victim-offender panels) that permit victims and offenders to encounter one another outside of the courtroom. The purpose of the encounter is to hold offenders accountable for their actions and to have offenders make reparation to their victims. First, in victim-offender reconciliation programs, "victims and offenders are given the opportunity to meet together with the assistance of a trained mediator to begin to resolve the conflict and construct their own approach to achieving justice."[9] Second, family group conferencing involves not only having the victim and offender meet with a mediator, but it includes the victim's and offender's families or support groups in the meeting. Third, a "victim-offender panel is made up of a group of victims and a group of offenders who are usually linked by a common kind of crime, although the particular crimes of which they were the perpetrators or offenders are not in common. In other words, where victim-offender reconciliation programs and family group conferencing meetings bring together offenders with their victims, victim-offender panels bring together groups of unrelated victims and offenders."[10] The book demonstrates that these programs are beneficial for victims and offenders alike.

Van Ness and Strong point out that the attrition rate in crime reporting, arrests, and convictions (i.e., only 1 out of 3 crimes is reported to the police, and for every 1,000 crimes, around 70 result in an arrest and about 35 result in a conviction) is a serious problem in America's current criminal justice system (a system based on retributive justice). The authors state that the reasons why restorative justice programs may be able to reduce this attrition rate. First, "restorative justice's emphasis on a community-government partnership in establishing safe communities is a strategy likely to increase the likelihood of crimes being reported and suspects identified, while simultaneously reducing the incidence of crime."[11] Second, "victims are more inclined to report crimes if they believe that the inconvenience of reporting and assisting with prosecution will be offset by recovery of their losses."[12]

Overall, Van Ness and Strong's work, *Restoring Justice,* persuasively argues the case for the United States to move from a criminal justice system based on retributive justice to a system based on restorative justice.

NOTES

1. Originally published as Louis Gesualdi, "Van Ness and Heetderks Strong's *Restoring Justice,*" *Journal of Contemporary Criminal Justice* 15, no. 3 (August 1999): 354-357.

2. Daniel Van Ness and Karen Heetderks Strong, *Restoring Justice* (Cincinnati, OH: Anderson, 1997), 42.

3. Ibid.
4. Ibid.
5. Ibid.
6. Ibid.
7. Ibid.
8. Ibid.
9. Ibid., 69.
10. Ibid., 74.
11. Ibid., 168.
12. Ibid.

Chapter Three

Look at *The Color of Justice*[1]

Samuel Walker, Cassia Spohn and Miriam DeLone's book, *The Color of Justice: Race, Ethnicity and Crime in America*, examines the American criminal justice system's treatment of racial and ethnic minorities (African Americans, Hispanic Americans, Asian Americans and Native Americans). The text analyzes the current research on police practices, court processing and sentencing, the death penalty, prisons and other correctional institutions. It indicates that even though Supreme Court decisions and statutory reforms have reduced blatant racism directed against racial minorities by criminal justice officials, the American criminal justice system is still characterized by racial and ethnic discrimination against minorities in certain situations or contexts.[2]

Walker, Spohn and DeLone provide persuasive evidence of police misconduct directed against racial and ethnic minorities. The authors show minorities, more likely than whites, are shot and killed, arrested, and victimized by the police. They point out that today's injustices suffered by minorities at the hands of the police are partially the result of discrimination against people of color.[3]

The Color of Justice maintains that racial discrimination continues in today's court processing and sentencing. The book points out that judges in some jurisdictions still impose harsher sentences on African American offenders who murder or rape whites and more lenient sentences on African Americans who victimize other African Americans. It indicates that judges in less serious cases tend to sentence African Americans to prison, while whites get probation. Furthermore, the text demonstrates that racial discrimination persists in decisions regarding bail, charging, jury selection and the juvenile justice system.[4]

Walker, Spohn and DeLone present studies that demonstrate the continuance of racial discrimination in the application of the death penalty in the criminal justice system. They note the race of the offender and race of the victim influence the judges' and jurors' willingness to impose the death penalty. The authors point out those offenders who murder whites are more likely sentenced to death than offenders who murder African Americans. They also indicate that African Americans convicted of murdering whites receive the death penalty more often than whites who murder other whites. [5]

The Color of Justice in its analysis of race and crime in America maintains that those who argue that racism does not exist in today's criminal justice system are misinformed. The book concludes that "the American criminal justice system has never been, and is not now, color blind."[6]

Walker, Spohn and DeLone's work, *The Color of Justice: Race, Ethnicity and Crime in America*, by its reporting of the discrimination against racial and ethnic minorities in the American criminal justice system, represents a peacemaking approach to criminology. Making one aware of this racial and ethnic discrimination is the first step toward ending such suffering and oppression of minorities.

NOTES

1. Originally published as Louis Gesualdi, "Walker, Spohn and Delone's *The Color of Justice,*" *Crime, Law and Social Change* 28, no. 4 (1997): 183-184.
2. Samuel Walker, Cassia Spohn and Miriam DeLone, *The Color of Justice: Race, Ethnicity and Crime in America* (New York: Wadsworth Publishing Company, 1996).
3. Ibid.
4. Ibid.
5. Ibid.
6. Ibid., 232.

Chapter Four

Bohm's *Deathquest*

A Brief Aspect[1]

Robert M. Bohm's *Deathquest: An Introduction to Theory and Practice of Capital Punishment in the United States* is a detailed, fact-based work on the death penalty (capital punishment) in America. The author discusses a history of the death penalty, presents the arguments for and against capital punishment, and investigates the cost of capital punishment. He also examines the miscarriages of justice in capital cases and discrimination in the administration of the death penalty.[2]

Deathquest traces the history of capital punishment in the United States. The book indicates that more than 19,000 executions have been performed in the United States under civil authority since 1608. It shows that nearly all of the people executed in America have been male adults.[3] Moreover, the text points out that "more capital offenders were executed during the 1930s than in any other decade in American history; the average was 167 executions per year."[4]

Bohm examines the arguments and counterarguments employed by proponents and opponents of the death penalty. He notes that many Americans believe that either threat of execution or executions themselves prevent other people from committing capital crimes. However, the author shows that there is no scientific evidence demonstrating capital punishment having any deterrent effect. *Deathquest* compares the costs of administering the death penalty to the costs of life imprisonment without opportunity for parole (LWOP). The book presents proof clearly showing that capital punishment in the United States is always more expensive than LWOP. Bohn describes incidents of wrongful convictions and wrongful executions. The author, in presenting the data, shows that nearly 500 defendants who were convicted of capital cases

15

in the 20th century were later found to be innocent. He points out that among "the innocent people wrongfully convicted were 23 people who were wrongfully executed." [5]

The book discusses the errors that occur that lead to wrongful convictions in capital cases. These errors involved shoddy investigation by the police, eyewitness misidentification, perjury by prosecution witnesses, false confessions, guilty pleas by innocent defendants, and the poor quality of legal representation in capital cases. [6]

Bohm demonstrates that the procedural reforms in the criminal justice system that have been implemented since 1972 have not eliminated discriminatory practices of the death penalty. He found that black defendants, as an outcome of discrimination, were more likely to receive the death penalty than whites. [7] The author also indicates that "a person convicted of aggravated murder of a white, whether the killer was a black or a white, was more likely to receive the death penalty than was a person of either race convicted of aggravated murder of a black." [8]

Robert M. Bohm's research in *Deathquest: An Introduction to Theory and Practice of Capital Punishment in the United States* represents a peacemaking approach to criminology by providing data that do not support many popular notions of the death penalty.

NOTES

1. Originally published as Louis Gesualdi, "Bohm's *Deathquest: An Introduction to the Theory of Capital Punishment in the United States,*" *Crime, Law and Social Change* 31, no. 2 (March 1999): 154-155.

2. Robert Bohm, *Deathquest: An Introduction to Theory and Practice of Capital Punishment in the United States* (Cincinnati: Anderson Publishing Company, 1999).

3. Ibid., 2.

4. Ibid., 7.

5. Ibid., 128.

6. Bohm, *Deathquest: An Introduction to Theory and Practice of Capital Punishment in the United States*.

7. Ibid., 156.

8. Ibid., 157.

Chapter Five

Youth Living in Poverty [1]

Terry Williams and William Kornblum's ethnographic work, *Growing Up Poor,* looks at the lives of 900 teenagers in New York City, Cleveland, Louisville and Meridian (Mississippi). Based on the teenagers' own accounts (through the use of in depth interviews), the authors indicate how some teens escape poverty and how others give up trying. These teenagers are from white neighborhoods that are sliding into poverty as traditional blue-collar jobs fade away and from black and Hispanic neighborhoods where unemployment and poverty have long been a way of life. [2]

Growing Up Poor investigates the bad choices made by many youth from impoverished areas. These choices, which often make poverty a permanent situation for these adolescents, include teen pregnancy and early parenthood, work in the underground economy (prostitution, street hustles, drug dealings and other criminal activities) and gang membership. Furthermore, this research describes the teenagers' work experience, their school and athletic achievements, and for some teens their positive adult influences. [3]

Williams and Kornblum demonstrate that bad choices made by many of these teenagers are a result of being born poor and having few caring adults around. In other words, the authors point out that a chief problem of many young people living in poverty, besides limited economic opportunities, is that adult influences are lacking or are of the type that steer teenagers toward the underground economy and other anti-social activities. Throughout the book, the authors provide data that show how some adults have directly or indirectly influenced many teens to make bad choices. [4]

The authors describe how some of these young people managed to escape poverty because of caring adults. These caring adults include parents, teachers, coaches, youth workers, spiritual guides and employers. These individuals not only provided economic opportunities for these youth but also instilled values and motivation which enabled these teens to escape a dead-end existence.[5]

Williams and Kornblum support a peacemaking approach to criminology by concluding that new generations of poor adolescents can be prevented from making bad choices and living a dead-end existence. They successfully argue that failure by the government and/or businesses to develop and maintain programs which offer employment opportunities and positive adult supervision and guidance for disadvantaged youth will only produce higher rates of teenage pregnancy, more anti-social teenage behavior, and ever-increasing involvement of young people in the world of illegal hustles.[6]

The description of the teenagers in *Growing Up Poor* provides great insight into the lives of poor youth throughout the United States. Williams and Kornblum's research points out the limited choices that poor youth have as an outcome of few economic opportunities along with a lack of caring adults. *Growing Up Poor* provides a wealth of detailed information on poverty and the problems inherent in escaping such a lifestyle.

NOTES

1. Originally published as Louis Gesualdi, "Williams and Kornblum's *Growing Up Poor*: A Review," *Teaching Sociology* 16, no. 2 (April 1988).
2. Terry Williams and William Kornblum, *Growing Up Poor* (Lexington, MA: Lexington Books, 1988).
3. Ibid.
4. Ibid.
5. Ibid.
6. Ibid.

Chapter Six

Steinberg's *Ethnic Myth*

An Explanation[1]

Stephen Steinberg, in *The Ethnic Myth,* argues that "ethnic patterns" or values attributed to one's cultural group must be related to the larger social matrix in which they are embedded. Traits which are often considered "ethnic" may well be more directly related to class, locality and other social conditions. Steinberg's investigation of economic and historical factors affecting the behavior of various American minority groups provides insight into why some immigrants succeed while others fail.[2]

Steinberg's approach is an exploration of social forces which influence the form and content of ethnicity, and he studies three sets of problems: 1) the viability of ethnic identities now and in the future, 2) the rates of mobility and success experienced by different ethnic groups, and 3) the social class character of racial and ethnic conflict. In each instance, the cultural-value explanations that have been commonly advanced over the years are challenged by Steinberg in his establishment of the historical and material bases of the "ethnic patterns."[3]

The viability of ethnic identities has always been in jeopardy according to Steinberg, because immigrant communities have lacked control over the economic base and the public schools. First, most immigrants were forced to go outside the ethnic community for employment. This is even truer of the children of immigrants whose mobility is dependent on their gaining access to the occupational structure of the larger society. Second, the public schools were designed to function as the chief instrument for assimilating and for producing a common culture of the mélange of immigrant groups that were pouring into the country. Steinberg, in defending this argument, notes that profound changes have occurred among American ethnic groups over the

19

past century—the loss of the mother tongue and most other core elements of immigrant culture, the dispersion of immigrant communities, the considerable economic and occupational mobility over several generations, the erosion and atrophy of ethnic cultures, the decline of religion which once buttressed ethnicity, the cultural convergence of the various ethnic sub societies, and accelerating rates of ethnic and religious intermarriages. Ethnic identities have been crumbling and the author states that the socio-economic conditions in America never promised genuine and lasting pluralism.[4]

In his discussion of the rates of mobility and success experienced by different ethnic groups, Steinberg states that there has been a tendency by social scientists to use the response of the poor, who explain their poverty as a cultural value. He points out that minority groups do not get ahead or lag behind on the basis of their cultural values, but rather they are born into a given station in life and adopt values that are consonant with their circumstances and life chances. In other words, "to the extent that lower class ethnics seem to live according to a different set of values, this is primarily a cultural manifestation of their being trapped in poverty."[5]

Finally, blatant racism on the part of white ethnics according to Steinberg should not be taken at face value. Steinberg argues that it is far from clear that white resistance to integration (conflict) stems from race prejudice per se. The white ethnics' fears of integration are not rooted in prejudice (that is superstition and irrationality) so much as in the realities of a class society. Steinberg points out that what is feared by white ethnics is not racial mixing but reduced property values, and deteriorating neighborhoods and schools, which are associated with blacks. Thus, what exists is a conflict between the racial have-nots and the ethnics who have a little and are afraid of losing that.[6]

Stephen Steinberg demonstrates that economic and social conditions create and maintain ethnic traits (cultural values), and ethnic traits are not the primary element in explaining behavioral characteristics. Cultural values are more a dependent than an independent variable.[7]

Steinberg's *The Ethnic Myth* supports peacemaking criminology. Peacemaking criminology points out that more research, like Steinberg's work, needs to be done in examining socioeconomic conditions such as economic inequalities, imbalance of power, poverty, unemployment, underemployment and relative deprivation—in income, housing, healthcare and education.

NOTES

1. Originally published as Louis Gesualdi, "Steinberg's *Ethnic Myth: Race, Ethnicity and Class*," *The Journal of Ethnic Studies* 11, no. 4 (1984): 132-134.
2. Stephen Steinberg, *The Ethnic Myth: Race, Ethnicity and Class in America* (Boston: Beacon Press, 1981).
3. Ibid.

4. Ibid.
5. Ibid.
6. Ibid.
7. Ibid.

Chapter Seven

A Review of Steinberg's *Turning Back*[1]

Stephen Steinberg's *Turning Back: The Retreat From Racial Justice in American Thought and Policy* examines social science writings on race relations over the past half century. The author shows how mainstream social science, with the exception of the decade of the 1960s, failed to confront racism and champion civil rights. He also indicates how many social scientists were not and are not willing to place responsibility for America's racial problems on political and economic institutions.[2] In agreement with Steinberg, Peacemaking Criminology argues that political and economic institutions in the United States are mainly responsible for suffering and oppression (in this case, racial oppression).

Turning Back criticizes social science research that attributes racial inequality (poverty) to different value systems. The book notes that ethnic and racial groups do differ in their aspirations and values, but these cultural differences are the result of historical and economic factors. It demonstrates that socioeconomic conditions create and maintain cultural values and that these values are not the primary factors in explaining behavioral characteristics. This work argues that cultural values are more a dependent than independent variable.[3]

Steinberg points out that in the United States the essence of racial oppression is "a racial division of labor, a system of occupational segregation that relegates most blacks to work in the least desirable job sector or that excludes them from job markets altogether."[4]

The author shows that blacks were restricted to the agricultural sector during the most expansive period of the industrial revolution in America (that is, from 1880 to 1930), and then they were evicted from rural America (as a result of the modernization of agriculture) and arrived in Northern cities at a time (after World War II) when manufacturing was beginning an irreversible decline.[5] He notes that racism, which restricted the access of black workers to jobs in declining industries, has also restricted black entry to new jobs in the expanding service sector.[6]

Turning Back indicates that the number of blacks below the poverty line has steadily increased over the past twenty years. The book notes that today's "blacks, who are 12 percent of the population, account for 29 percent of the poor, the same proportion as in 1960."[7] Furthermore, the work points out that nearly "half of all black children under age 18 are being raised in families below the poverty line, as compared to 16 percent of whites."[8]

Steinberg demonstrates that the United States' economic and political system, during the last one hundred thirty years, has failed for the most part to address racial inequality. He notes four lost opportunities in which this country could have wiped out social division and conflict.[9]

First, the promise of Reconstruction (forty acres and a mule promised to former slaves after the civil war) was not kept. The situation for African Americans in agriculture would have been different if the black farmer had the opportunity to establish himself as an independent owner rather than a sharecropper or tenant farmer.[10]

Second, between 1880 and 1920 "the nation missed a unique opportunity to incorporate blacks into the mainstream of the economy at a time when there was rapid growth and a dire shortage of labor."[11] During this time, 24 million immigrants arrived to the United States, and very few blacks from the South migrated to the North where the industrial jobs were.[12] Steinberg indicates the reason why few blacks migrated to the North was that a "color line, maintained by employers and workers alike, barred blacks from virtually the entire industrial sector."[13]

Third, with the Second World War, Northern labor markets opened up to blacks which stimulated the migration of Southern blacks.[14] Steinberg also indicated that many white and black Americans expected that blacks would be rewarded for their services to WWII. However, the federal government was not "a champion of black rights during the postwar period" (that is, the 1950s).[15]

Fourth, the United States failed "to follow through on the momentous changes wrung out of white society by the civil rights movement" of the 1960s.[16] Steinberg notes that even after the passage of civil rights acts of the 1960s racism still exists as "blacks continue to lag behind whites in terms of major social indicators."[17] Specifically, gaps between blacks and whites in incomes and living standards have widened in the last thirty years as an outcome of America's political and economic institutions. In short, the United States has failed to incorporate African Americans into the economic mainstream during the thirteen decades since the abolition of slavery.[18]

Stephen Steinberg successfully shows that through most of it history the United States has failed to address the racial divisions and inequalities that are the legacy of slavery. Furthermore, he argues that the social sciences, with the exception of the 1960s, failed to deal with issues of race and racism.

NOTES

1. Originally published as Louis Gesualdi, "Steinberg's *Turning Back*: A Review," *The Humanist* 57, no. 4 (1997): 45.

2. Stephern Steinberg, *Turning Back: The Retreat from Racial Justice in American Thought and Policy* (Boston: Beacon Press, 1995).

3. Ibid.

4. Ibid., 79-80.

5. Steinberg, *Turning Back: The Retreat from Racial Justice in American Thought and Policy* (Boston: Beacon Press, 1995), 183.

6. Ibid.

7. Ibid., 213.

8. Ibid.

9. Steinberg, *Turning Back: The Retreat from Racial Justice in American Thought and Policy*.

10. Ibid.

11. Ibid., 210.

12. Steinberg, *Turning Back: The Retreat from Racial Justice in American Thought and Policy*, 209.

13. Ibid.

14. Steinberg, *Turning Back: The Retreat from Racial Justice in American Thought and Policy*, 211.

15. Ibid.

16. Ibid.

17. Steinberg, *Turning Back: The Retreat from Racial Justice in American Thought and Policy*, 212.

18. Steinberg, *Turning Back: The Retreat from Racial Justice in American Thought and Policy*.

Chapter Eight

The Black Single Female Headed Family and Crime[1]

Some social scientists, such as Daniel P. Moynihan[2] and James Q. Wilson,[3] have argued that the black single female headed family is deficient in providing the discipline and habits necessary for personality development in African American youth. They claim that the said requirements for personality development can only be provided by the father, and they view the black single-female-headed household as a major cause of America's high crime rates. However, the data refute this assessment.

U.S. Census data indicate that from 1970 to 1992, the percentage of children under eighteen years old living only with their mother increased from 7.8 percent to 18 percent among whites and from 29 percent to 58 percent among blacks.[4] Meanwhile, victimization reports from the Bureau of Justice Statistics show that in 1973, one in three Americans reported experiencing some form of property crime or violence during the preceding six months, and by 1992, the figure had dropped to one in four.[5] Likewise, FBI uniform crime reports show that the murder rate dropped from approximately 10 per 100,000 persons in 1973 to 8.2 per 100,000 persons in 1995.[6] In other words, the percentage of single female headed households among blacks and whites has increased at the same time property and violent crime rates—including the murder rate—have decreased. Logically speaking, if the black single female headed household is a major cause of America's high crime rates, these rates would have increased, not decreased.

These statistics alone refute Moynihan and Wilson's assessment of what causes crime. However, there are other statistics which clear the name of black single mothers.

Contrary to the picture presented by rates of arrests, convictions and imprisonment, there is no significant difference in the overall illegal drug use between whites and blacks.[7] Although blacks constitute 35 percent of arrests for drug possession, 55 percent of convictions and 74 percent of prison sentences, this group accounts for only 13 percent of the illegal drug use in the United States.[8] There exist studies that point out the disparities in drug arrests and prison sentences between blacks and whites in America and indicate that racial discrimination by the criminal justice system accounts for these higher arrest rates and prison sentences cited for African Americans. These works demonstrate that racial discrimination operates, as it has historically, in excessive policing of black areas, decisions regarding bail and charging, and sentences imposed by judges.[9] Therefore, since blacks have a higher percentage of single female headed households than whites and since there is no significant difference in illegal drug use between whites and blacks, the black single female headed household is obviously not a major cause of illegal drugs used in the United States.

Second, whites make up 80 percent of the youth population in the United States, while blacks make up 16 percent. Yet, according to the U.S. Department of Justice, whites make up 80 percent of all runaways and commit 81 percent of all arsons, 81 percent of vandalisms, 94 percent of DUIs, 93 percent of liquor law violations, and 88 percent of drunkenness, while blacks make up only 16 percent of all runaways and commit 17 percent of all arsons, 17 percent of vandalisms, 4 percent of DUIs, 4 percent of liquor law violations, and 10 percent of drunkenness.[10] As one can see, the arrest rates of black youth coincide with or are lower than their proportion of the general youth population. If the black single female headed household plays a major role in crime, black youth should have much higher rates compared to their proportion in the general youth population—that is, much higher than 16 percent.

Third, let's consider that white-collar crimes are committed mostly by whites from the middle and upper classes and not by the poor and working classes, which contain a high percentage of black single-female-headed households. Research (discussed more in upcoming chapters) points out that white-collar crimes do significantly more harm to society than all street crimes put together and that laws are not as strongly enforced against white-collar crimes as they are against street crimes. For example, the total monetary damage from white-collar crimes is estimated to be $231 billion a year, while street crimes are estimated at only $10 billion a year. Each year, an estimated 200,000 people die and 20 million people are injured from white-collar crimes (outcomes of unsafe workplaces and unsafe products). This far exceeds the 20,000 murders and 850,000 assaults (that is, street crimes) committed each year in the United States. And while white-collar crimes are widespread, relatively few white-collar criminals are ever arrested or prosecuted. These criminals commit crimes repeatedly and, when apprehended, are treated with far more leniency than street-crime offenders. America's arrest and imprisonment rates do not accurately reflect the high number of dangerous crimes committed mostly by the well-off.[11] So, even though blacks represent a disproportionately high number of prison inmates compared to their percentage in the general population, black single female headed households have not played a role.

Given the data, then, it follows that we must look outside the family structure for the causes of crime. Peacemaking Criminology maintains that instead of blaming black single mothers, it would be wiser to direct our research at examining socioeconomic conditions, such as economic inequality, imbalances of power, poverty, unemployment, underemployment, and relative deprivation—in income, housing, health care, and education.

NOTES

1. Originally published as Louis Gesualdi, "Don't Blame Mom for Crime," *The Humanist,* (May/June 1998): 3.

2. Daniel P. Moynihan, "Defining Deviance Down," *The American Scholar* (Winter 1993).

3. James, Q. Wilson, "What to do about Crime," *Commentary* (September 1994).

4. Richard P. Appelbaum and William Chambliss, *Sociology: A Brief Introduction* (New York: Longman, 1997), *U.S. Bureau of the Census*, Washington, D. C.: Government Printing Office, 1993 and 1970, and J. R. Eschleman and B.G. Cashion, *Sociology* (Boston: Little, Brown and Company, 1985).

5. B.J.S. Bulletin, *Bureau of Justice Statistics Bulletin, Criminal Victimization,* 1993, 1989, and Richard P. Appelbaum and William J. Chambliss, *Sociology: A Brief Introduction.*

6. M.R. Rand, J.P. Lynch, and D. Cantor, "Criminal Victimization, 1973-95," *Bureau of Justice of Statistics, National Crime Victimization Survey,* 1997.

7. P. Elikann, *The Tough on Crime Myth* (New York: Insight Books, 1996): 58.

8. Ibid., 58.

9. P. Elikann, *The Tough on Crime Myth*, 1996, and S. Walker, C. Spohn, and M. DeLone, *The Color of Justice: Race, Ethnicity, and Crime in America* (California: Wadsworth Publishing, Company, 1996).

10. H.N. Snyder, "Arrests of Youth 1990," *Juvenile Justice Bulletin, U.S. Department of Justice,* January 1992.

11. V. Kappeler, M. Blumberg and G. Potter, *The Mythology of Crime and Criminal Justice* (Illinois: Waveland Press, Incorporated, 1996) and J. Reiman, *The Rich Get Richer and the Poor Get Prison* (Boston: Allyn and Bacon, 1998).

Chapter Nine

Popular Notions of Affirmative Action

A Criticism[1]

It has been commonly preached that the United States is a great meritocracy and that hard work yields success. Affirmative action has been popularly believed to undermine the grand meritocracy that is the United States (that is, a magnificent meritocracy of America is not succeeding today because of affirmative action). Moreover, it is popularly believed that white males are deprived of jobs due to affirmative action. This chapter examines these notions of affirmative action and presents data that do not support the above opinions.

Affirmative action is not the cause of a failing meritocracy in America because the United States has never been a true meritocracy.[2] Bernstein,[3] Steinberg[4] and Cocco[5] indicate that throughout the history of the U. S. many educational and occupational opportunities have not been given to the "best qualified."

Opportunities in America were never truly based on merit. Past research points out the following facts. First, colleges have accepted and accept athletes, violinists, rural or blue collar applicants, class leaders and alumni children who score lower than others. For instance, the University of California Medical School took 16 whites with scores lower than Alan Bakee's when he sued the University for taking blacks with lower scores. Second, civil service has given and gives preference to veterans. Third, many white men have been and still are given jobs not due to merit but due to relatives and friends being at key positions in the workplace. This is known as the old boy network.[6]

More studies demonstrate that a generation after affirmative action began white males still receive society's greatest rewards and not as an outcome of

31

merit. First, according to data by the U. S. Glass Ceiling Commission, blacks and women who are managers and professionals are paid less than their white male counterparts in every industry, even when people with equal education and experience are compared. Second, a 1990 Business Week Study found that a woman with an M. B. A. from a top- 20 business school earned an average of $54,749 the year after graduation compared with $64,400 for men. Third, black men who work full-time, year round, earn about 72 percent of what white men do; the ratio for white women is about 70 percent. For black women it is about 62 percent. Fourth, Labor Department data show women are paid less than men in every occupational group from janitor to judge.[7]

Research shows the existence of a system, past and present, of occupational segregation in the United States. This system relegated and still relegates most blacks to work in the least desirable job sector or excludes them from job markets altogether.[8] Blacks were restricted to the agricultural sector during the most expansive period of the industrial revolution in America (that is, from 1880 to 1930), were evicted from rural America (as a result of modernization of agriculture) and arrived in Northern cities at a time (after World War II) when manufacturing was beginning an irreversible decline. Racism which restricted the access of black workers to jobs in declining industries is also restricting black entry into new jobs in today's service sector.[9] In other words, blacks in general, did not and still do not have access to many types of jobs and this lack of access is not due to a lack of qualifications or merit but due to racism.[10]

In short, the research discussed above does not support the notion that a magnificent meritocracy is not succeeding in the U. S. because of affirmative action. The data show that American society has never been a true meritocracy.

White males are not being deprived of jobs due to affirmative action. The research verifies that whites, males in particular, are still preferred in job hiring over black men and women, in general, in spite of over twenty-five years of affirmative action.[11]

The research indicates that year after year from 1960 to 1995, the unemployment rates of blacks have been double the rates of whites and shows that today, 33% of all blacks still live in poverty (same as the 1960s) while 10% of all whites are poor.[12] Research also points out the following occupational representations. First, African Americans today still have more than their share of janitorial jobs and cleaning up after others, which have been traditional "black" positions. Second, the position where blacks have the greatest representation tend to be jobs that whites are unwilling to take (such as hotel maids and housemen, and nursing aids and orderlies) as well as some jobs at lower civil service positions (correctional officers and postal clerks). African-Americans in the 1990s performed repetitious office tasks (data entry keyers and telephone operators), and they fill in at high-turnover occupations (security guards and taxicab drivers). Third, in a few instances, the occupations offering expanded opportunities (bus drivers and social workers) to African-Americans are ones administering to clients that have become disproportionately black. Fourth, in the 1990s, the proportion of white men who are self employed is 7.4%, while the proportion of black men who are self employed is only 3.0%. Overall, it is clear that blacks have not taken away jobs from white men.[13] Continuing on this theme that white men are not being deprived of jobs due to affirmative action, other studies indicate the following information: First, a "generation after affirmative action began, more than 95% of top executives are white males."[14] Second, a study of Stanford business school graduates discovered that ten years after graduation, 16 percent of the men were CEOs versus 2 percent of the women.[15] Third, a recent "Urban Institute study of equally qualified blacks and whites in Washington and Chicago showed that whites were offered jobs three times as often as blacks, were interviewed longer and steered to better jobs."[16] Overall, these data do not support the notion that white males are being deprived of jobs due to affirmative action.

After examining and analyzing the above data, I argue that affirmative action is necessary based on the following reasons: First, affirmative action "asks only that qualified minority applicants for jobs or college places be considered."[17] Second, the data presented in this chapter do not support the popular notions of affirmative action. The United States has never been a true meritocracy, and white men are not deprived as a result of affirmative action. Third, today, blacks and women, in general, are still being discriminated against in jobs, and affirmative action is their only network to possibly overcome this discrimination.

Peacemaking Criminology points out that other acts and programs need to be developed and supported in order for affirmative action to successfully correct past and present discrimination. Such acts and programs would involve the development and protection of basic human rights. Basic human rights include full and steady employment, a good standard of living income and full health care coverage for everyone. These basic rights do not exist in the United States today. Affirmative action would be almost meaningless if unemployment, underemployment, poverty and a lack of health care continue to exist in this country. In conclusion, Peacemaking Criminology indicates that the development and protection of basic human rights, including affirmative action, are needed in America for all forms of discrimination to end and for human beings to have full, productive, healthy and creative lives.

NOTES

1. Originally published as Louis Gesualdi, "Popular Notions of Affirmative Action: A Criticism," *Sociological Viewpoints* (Fall 2001): 55-57.

2. Stephen Steinberg, *Turning Back: The Retreat from Racial Justice in American Thought and Policy* (Boston: Beacon Press, 1995).

3. B. Bernstein, "Qualifying for Affirmative Action," *New York Newsday,* August 9, 1995.

4. Steinberg, *Turning Back: The Retreat from Racial Justice in American Thought and Policy.*

5. M arie Cocco, "White Men Deprived? Name a Couple of Dozen?" *New York Newsday,* March 30, 1995.

6. Bernstein, "Qualifying for Affirmative Action," August 9, 1995 and Steinberg, *Turning Back: The Retreat from Racial Justice in American Thought and Policy.*

7. Cocco, "White Men Deprived? Name a Couple of Dozen?"

8. Steinberg, *Turning Back: The Retreat from Racial Justice in American Thought and Policy,* 79-80.

9. Ibid., 183.

10. Ibid.

11. Bernstein, "Qualifying for Affirmative Action," Cocco, "White Men Deprived? Name a Couple of Dozen?," and A. Hacker, *Two Nations: Black and White, Separate, Hostile, Unequal,* (New York: Charles Scribner's Sons, 1992).

12. Richard Appelbaum and William Chambliss, *Sociology: A Brief Introduction* (New York: Longman, 1997) and Hacker, *Two Nations: Black and White, Separate, Hostile, Unequal.*

13. Hacker, *Two Nations: Black and White, Separate, Hostile, Unequal,* 107-133.

14. Cocco, "White Men Deprived? Name a Couple of Dozen?"

15. Ibid.

16. Bernstein, "Qualifying for Affirmative Action."

17. Ibid.

Chapter Ten

Kappeler, Blumberg and Potter's
The Mythology of Crime
and Criminal Justice

A Brief Aspect[1]

Victor E. Kappeler, Mark Blumberg and Gary Potter's *The Mythology of Crime and Criminal Justice* questions the many widespread beliefs of deviance, crime and criminal justice in the United States. Their book shows how different crime related problems and issues (such as, organized crime, police work, illegal drugs, incarceration rates and capital punishment) have been twisted into myths.[2]

The text analyzes the development of specific myths of crime. They discuss the common techniques employed by the media, law enforcement personnel, and government officials to manipulate information and construct crime myths. Such practices include creating criminal stereotypes; interjecting personal opinion into media presentation without factual basis; collecting opinions of others that closely match the media, law enforcement, and government officials' viewpoints; using value-laden terms to describe crime, criminals, or victims; presenting certain facts and not others; presenting supposedly factual information with undocumented sources of authority; interjecting facts that are unrelated to an issue; and interviewing one or two authorities on a subject and presenting their comments as generalized expert opinion on a topic.[3]

The authors examine and debunk many public myths regarding crime and criminal justice. Some of the myths challenged by the authors include the following:

Myth—A majority of missing children are abducted by strangers. Reality—The official numbers of missing children in the United States not only include stranger abductions, but also teenage runaways and parental abductions. Runaways actually make up almost 98% of the missing children, whereas parental abductions make up the remaining 2%. The rest (a fraction of 1%) are abducted by strangers. Numerically, fewer than 300 children are abducted by strangers yearly.[4]

Myth—White-collar crimes cause less damage (both economic and physical) than do traditional street crimes. Reality—The total monetary damage from white-collar crime is estimated to be $231 billion a year, whereas street crime is estimated to $10 billion a year. In addition, each year, an estimated 200,000 people die and 20,000,000 more are seriously injured from white-collar crime that is an outcome of unsafe workplaces and unsafe products. In contrast, approximated 23,000 murders and 850,000 assaults are committed in the streets each year in the United States. Street crime, according to the authors, is less of a threat, less of a danger, and less of a burden to society than white-collar crime. They also point out that (a) white-collar crime is widespread and few white-collar criminals are ever arrested or prosecuted; (b) these criminals commit crimes repeatedly and with great frequency; and (c) when apprehended, white-collar criminals are treated with far more consideration and leniency than traditional offenders.[5]

Myth—Intravenous drug dealers will not alter their behavior to protect themselves from the AIDS virus. Many drug users, the authors indicate, are willing to change their behavior. Furthermore, they indicate that many intravenous drug users have taken steps to reduce their risk of HIV infection such as no longer sharing injection equipment, reducing the number of persons with whom they share needles, only using sterile needles, cleaning injection equipment prior to use, or reducing their levels of drug use.[6]

Myth—Illegal drugs are so dangerous that legal prohibition is justified. The authors place the issue of harm from illegal drugs in context and examine the drugs that have elicited the strongest reaction from lawmakers and law enforcers, namely heroin, cocaine and marijuana. The authors point out that drug-related deaths are (a) relatively infrequent, despite popular impressions, and (b) more directly attributable to drug laws than to the drugs themselves. They indicate that the number of people who die each year from the consumption of all illegal drugs (approximately 3,600) pales in comparison to the number of deaths on a yearly basis from two legal drugs, alcohol (approximately 200,000) and tobacco (approximately 320,000). The authors conclude that drug laws make the drug problem in the United States worse. They further suggest that there are possible benefits from the legalization of drugs. They argue that (a) repealing drug laws will save at least $10 billion a year in law enforcement, (b) organized crime groups would be dealt a severe setback, and (c) the quality of life for millions of drug users would improve greatly if legal controls were removed.

Myth—The American criminal justice system is lenient. The authors conclude quite to the contrary. They examine both cross-national and longitudinal data with respect to punishment practices. Specifically, incarceration rates and practices with respect to the use of capital punishment are analyzed. In both cases, the work shows that the United States is not more lenient than other comparable societies. As is well known, the United States has the highest incarceration rates of all Western democracies (currently in excess of 500:100,000). The United States is the only Western democracy that still uses the death penalty and is among a small minority of nations in which juveniles can be executed for crimes. After presenting and analyzing statistics with respect to the number of jail inmates, sentenced federal and state prisoners, and probationers and parolees, the work argues that America's criminal justice system is quite punitive by contemporary standards.[7]

Myth—Serial killers account for a substantial percentage (as large as 20%) of all murders annually committed in the United States. Actually, the authors note that serial murders remain an extreme fringe of American crime. They show that such murders account for possibly 2% or 3% of American homicides and certainly not the 20% of all murders that is constantly cited in the popular press.[8]

Myth—Policing is an extremely dangerous occupation. The authors show that not only are the killings of police officers relatively rare events in the United States, but these killings have declined from a high of 132 officers in 1974 (1:4500) to 76 by 1994 (1:11,000).[9] Furthermore, the authors point out that the

> Risk associated with police work has declined despite the restrictions that have been placed on police use of firearms, the increase in the rate of violent crime, the proliferation of semiautomatic weapons on the streets of American cities, the war on drugs, and the increase in the level of gang-related violence that has occurred in many communities.[10]

The Mythology of Crime and Criminal Justice shows that overall, America's rate of street crime (theft, assault, murder) has been decreasing since the 1970s. The book successfully explains that the American crime wave (out of control rates of violent crime) did not and does not exist. Moreover, this work points out that crime, contrary to popular notion, is committed, for the most part, in social settings by unarmed people who are relatives, friends and acquaintances of the victims. This text also makes clear that most crime is minor, and it demonstrates very little crime results in serious injury.[11]

The authors make evident that white-collar crimes are a substantially greater hazard to the public than street crimes. White-collar crimes include

crimes against the consumer (fraud, unsafe products), bribery and environmental crimes (pollution, unsafe workplaces). Kappeler, Blumberg and Potter state that "all other forms of criminal behavior in society do not begin to
equal the costs, in terms of both dollars and lives," of white-collar crimes. [12]
Furthermore, the authors in their analysis of white-collar crimes and street
crimes verify the bias against the poor that exists within America's criminal
justice system. [13]

The Mythology of Crime and Criminal Justice indicates that the excessive
concern by American society with street crimes overlooks more serious social problems (such as white-collar crimes, teenage runaways, and children
abused at the hands of their relatives). The book supports a peacemaking
approach to crime by concluding that such excessive concern with street
crimes by the American public leads to unnecessary and unjust laws, harsher
punishments that do not work in dealing with crime, and misplaced social
resources. [14] This text also presents the following questions and problems that
are masked when American society focuses mainly on street crimes.

- What is the real extent of crime in America?
- Why is law enforcement unable to deal with crime?
- Is there true equity in our courts?
- What are the vested interests of the criminal justice industry?
- What spin-off crimes are caused by the drug war?
- Are injuries caused by the government's drug crop eradication programs?
- How much corruption of government officials results from drug criminal-
  ization?
- What percentage of the public demands vice-related services and prod-
  ucts?
- Is there a symbiotic relationship between government and corporate
  crime?
- Who pays the $231 billion price tag of corporate and white-collar crime? [15]

NOTES

1. Originally published as Louis Gesualdi, "Bohm's *Deathquest: An Introduction to the
Theory of Capital Punishment in the United States*," *Crime, Law and Social Change* 31, no. 2
(March 1999): 154-155.
2. Victor E. Kappeler, Mark Blumberg, Gary Potter, *The Mythology of Crime and Criminal
Justice,* 2nd ed. (Illinois: Waveland Press, 1996).
3. Ibid.
4. Ibid.
5. Ibid.
6. Ibid.
7. Ibid.
8. Ibid.
9. Ibid.

10. Ibid., 216.

11. Victor E. Kappeler, Mark Blumberg, and Gary Potter, *The Mythology of Crime and Criminal Justice* 3rd ed. (Illinois: Waveland Press, 2000).

12. Ibid., 141.

13. Kappeler, Blumberg and Potter, *The Mythology of Crime and Criminal Justice* 3rd ed.

14. Ibid.

15. Ibid., 307-308.

Chapter Eleven

A Look into Simon and Hagan's
White-Collar Deviance[1]

David R. Simon and Frank E. Hagan's *White-Collar Deviance* is an in depth examination of white-collar wrongdoing of all types and forms. Their work discusses the economic and political aspects of white-collar deviance. It also analyzes the semblance and relationships between white-collar offenses and the actions of organized criminal syndicates. Furthermore, Simon and Hagan's book proposes changes in America's social system in order to properly deal with white-collar deviance.[2]

The authors use the National White-Collar Crime Center definition of white-collar crime in defining white-collar deviance. White-collar deviance is defined as follows: "Planned illegal or unethical acts of deception committed by an individual or organization, usually during the course of legitimate occupational activity by persons of high or respectable social status for personal or organizational gain that violate fiduciary responsibility or public trust."[3] Such deviance includes corporate crimes, government crimes, political corruption, and crimes in the professions, among others.

White-Collar Deviance indicates that even though corporate criminal violations cause a great deal more physical, financial and moral harm than street crimes in American society, the penalties for such corporate violations are totally lacking. Penalties that do exist contribute no deterrent to corporate crimes (such crimes include antitrust, advertising and pollution law violations, unsafe workplaces and unsafe products). The book points out that only about two percent of corporate crime cases end in incarceration.[4]

Simon and Hagan investigate the conditions of the global economy that produce white-collar deviance. The authors show how an advantageous few own much of corporate America and have extreme power over government administrations. They successfully argue that the centralization of wealth and power in the hands of such a few has given rise to a host of white-collar wrongdoings. Moreover, Simon and Hagan demonstrate that the people most adversely affected by white-collar wrongdoings tend to be the poorest members of their societies. [5]

The text indicates that multinational oligopolistic conglomerates manage the U.S. and global economy. The presence of such conglomerates, as shown by Simon and Hagan's work, increases the probability of an abundance of hurtful economic practices. Such practices include the following: 1. Price fixing. 2. Fraud. 3. Price-gouging. 4. False advertising. 5. Mergers and acquisitions at the cost of job growth. 6. Movement of plants to foreign countries where labor expenses are a small part of their U.S. counterparts and many costly regulations can be effortlessly avoided. 7. Undemocratic power with the federal government, resulting in all kinds of corporate subsidies and tax breaks at the cost of the average taxpayer. [6]

White-Collar Deviance illustrates that the "security, in the form of classifying paramilitary operations hidden from public view, has become a way of life" for the U.S. government. [7] The book indicates that the federal government has made an unpleasant practice of utilizing public funds to reinforce private profit. Furthermore, it points out that the U.S. government has ignored human rights at home and also has a history of supporting foreign governments that enlist violent restraint of human rights. [8]

Simon and Hagan discuss the crimes of the U.S. Presidents and make clear that political corruption has existed in nearly every presidential administration. They make evident that the top five presidential eras for crime, corruption and scandal were those of James Buchanan, Ulysses Grant, Warren Harding, Richard Nixon and Ronald Reagan. [9]

The authors describe the harmful acts that are committed in the professions. For instance, they indicate that in the medical profession "unnecessary operations and medical malpractice may kill more people every year in the United States than crimes of violence." [10] Simon and Hagan state that a "House subcommittee estimates 2.4 million unnecessary surgical procedures per year, costing 4 billion dollars and causing nearly 12,000 deaths." [11]

White-Collar Deviance proves that "organized crime syndicates have long been useful to so-called legitimate corporations and certain government agencies and politicians who have a need of illegal goods and services that only crime syndicates can provide." [12] The text points out "the uses political organizations and government agencies (including the CIA) have found for the goods and services of organized crime syndicates." [13] It also indicates that "certain legitimate business and entertainment interests have long used crime syndicates for a variety of purposes." [14]

The text verifies that the causes of white-collar deviance come straight from the institutional organizations and the value system of the U.S. political economy. It recommends the following changes in American society for dealing with white-collar offenses: 1. Reconstruct big corporations democratically to satisfy human necessities. For instance, the book argues that the best way to extend democracy and community accountability is to have workers install their pension funds in the corporation until they own a majority of the company's stock. 2. Decrease the government's size in the United States. This decrease would involve the following: campaign finance reform, strong consideration and study of term limitations for senators and representatives, and cutting down all possible expenditures (such as corporate subsidies). 3. Bring about full employment. Attached to every job should be health and dental insurance, life insurance and family leave, and some system of day care for children of employees. 4. Establish a program of social reconstruction. There is a necessity for better schools and smaller classes, more family doctors, nurses, teachers, computers in education and in homes, libraries, and drug-treatment facilities.[15] These recommendations exemplify a peacemaking approach to crime.

The authors point out that white-collar deviance holds many negative outcomes for society. These outcomes include high prices, dangerous products, unsafe work conditions, pollution, and the increased motivation to commit harmful acts on the part of the working and lower classes.[16]

NOTES

1. Originally published as Louis Gesualdi, "Simon and Hagan's *White-Collar Deviance:* A Review," *Journal of Contemporary Criminal Justice* 16, no. 4 (November 2000): 457-459.
2. David R. Simon and Frank E. Hagan, *White-Collar Deviance* (Boston: Allyn and Bacon, 1999).
3. Ibid., 6.
4. Simon and Hagan, *White-Collar Deviance.*
5. Ibid.
6. Ibid.
7. Ibid., 55.
8. Simon and Hagan, *White-Collar Deviance.*
9. Ibid.
10. Ibid., 80.
11. Ibid.
12. Simon and Hagan, *White-Collar Deviance,* 120.
13. Ibid.
14. Ibid.
15. Simon and Hagan, *White-Collar Deviance,* 164-165.
16. Simon and Hagan, *White-Collar Deviance.*

Chapter Twelve

A Brief Examination of Messner and Rosenfeld's *Crime and the American Dream*[1]

Steven F. Messner and Richard Rosenfeld's book *Crime and the American Dream* locates the source of U.S. crime rates in the values and behavior that are part of American society. High levels of crime in America are produced from cultural and social conditions that exist in this country.[2] The authors demonstrate that American culture being characterized by a combination of a strong emphasis on economic success and a weak emphasis on the legitimate means for the pursuit of success contributes to crime directly by encouraging to employ illegal means to achieve monetary goals.[3]

Crime and the American Dream describes the nature of the crime problem in the United States, and shows that there is something distinctive about crime and the response to crime in this country. The book presents evidence of the levels of homicides and robberies during the 20th century in the United States which substantially exceeds the highest rates of other industrial nations. With few exceptions, the lowest annual rates of homicides recorded in the United States over the past ninety years are greater than the highest rates found in other industrial nations. In addition, the book indicates that white collar crimes occur with great frequency in the U.S. and result in significant and collective harm.[4]

Messner and Rosenfeld explain how crime in the United States is reflected in and produced by an institutional structure dominated by the economy. They demonstrate that the dominant values of American culture (that is, achievement orientation, competitive individualism, and monetary success) support a social "environment highly conducive to criminal behavior."[5] The authors examine the universal dominance of the economy over the other social institutions (that is, the family, educational and political institutions) in America, and indicate that as an outcome of this dominance, the noneconomic institutions "have limited capacity to offer incentives and penalties for socially prescribed or proscribed behavior."[6] Messner and Rosenfeld point out that since these institutions are weak, Americans are exceptionally vulnerable to criminal behavior and that the pursuit of individual material success is more important than other values.[7]

Messner and Rosenfeld's work reviews the different theories in criminology and indicates that the high levels of serious crime in the U.S. result from the functions of the American social system. Their book points out the influences of the many social scientists (such as, Durkheim, de Tocqville, Marx, Bellah, Parsons and Mills) in shaping the authors' view about culture, social structure and crime. In particular, the work notes the influence of Merton in directly shaping Messner and Rosenfeld's explanation of America's high crime rates.[8]

Crime and the American Dream exemplifies a peacemaking analysis to crime. It provides a convincing argument that America's high levels of crime are basically outcomes of socio-economic conditions which exist in the United States.

NOTES

1. Originally published as Louis Gesualdi, "Messner and Rosenfeld's *Crime and the American Dream*: A Review, *Crime, Law and Social Change 26,* no.1 (March 1996): 96-97.
2. Steven, F. Messner and Richard Rosenfeld, *Crime and the American Dream,* California:Wadsworth Inc., 1994, p. 6.
3. Messner and Rosenfeld, *Crime and the American Dream,* 1994.
4. Ibid., p. 30.
5. Messner and Rosenfeld, *Crime and the American Dream,* 1994, p. 71.
6. Ibid., p. 87.
7. Messner and Rosenfeld, *Crime and the American Dream,* 1994.
8. Ibid.

Chapter Thirteen

Reiman's *The Rich Get Richer and the Poor Get Prison*

A Review[1]

Jeffrey Reiman's book *The Rich Get Richer and the Poor Get Prison: Ideology, Class and Criminal Justice* examines the harmful acts committed by the well-off. Such acts include embezzlement, bribery, computer crimes, crimes against the consumer (fraud, unsafe products), medical crimes, and environmental crimes (pollution, unsafe workplaces). The text, in its analysis of these harmful acts, points out the bias against the poor that exist within America's criminal justice system.[2]

The acts in which poor people harm others (theft, assault, murder) are treated as serious crimes, while harmful acts for which well-off people are responsible for are not treated as serious crimes (and many times are not treated as crimes at all). Harmful acts by the well-off oftentimes are a substantially greater hazard to the public than harmful acts by the poor. For instance, unsafe workplaces, unsafe products, medical crimes and pollution lead to far more misery, far more dying and disability, and cost more money than all the murders, aggravated assaults and thefts that are reported each year by the FBI.[3]

The criminal justice system tends to treat well-off offenders who are guilty of fraud, embezzlement, bribery and computer crimes more kindly than poor offenders who are guilty of nonviolent property crime. Well-off offenders are less likely to be arrested, prosecuted and incarcerated than poor offenders, even when they have committed the same offense.[4]

Reiman makes the following recommendations to protect the public from crime and advance justice.

47

- Policies need to be developed to eliminate poverty.
- Criminal justice needs to establish and execute punishments that fit the hurtfulness of the offense without regard to the class of the offender.
- American society needs to make lawful the production and sale of illicit drugs and deal with addiction as a medical challenge.
- Rehabilitation programs need to be developed in order to promote personal responsibility.
- Ex-offenders need to be offered training and a chance to succeed as law-abiding citizens.
- The range in which police officers, prosecutors, and judges exercise discretion needs to be restricted, and the development of policies to hold these law enforcers liable to the public for their decisions is necessary.
- American society has to enact a more just apportioning of wealth and income and to make equal opportunity a reality for everyone.[5]

Reiman's book *The Rich Get Richer and the Poor Get Prison: Ideology, Class and Criminal Justice* exemplifies peacemaking criminology. His book presents a humanistic and scientific approach to the study of crime. It shows the failure of the criminal justice system in reducing the large amount of dangerous offenses committed in American society.

NOTES

1. Originally published as Louis Gesualdi, "Reiman's *The Rich Get Richer and the Poor Get Prison,* " *Crime, Law and Social Change 31,* no. 2 (March 1999): 152-153.
2. Jeffrey Reiman, *The Rich Get Richer and the Poor Get Prison: Ideology, Class and Criminal Justice,* Boston: Allyn and Bacon, 1998.
3. Ibid.
4. Ibid.
5. Ibid.

Chapter Fourteen

Rosoff, Pontell and Tillman's
Profit without Honor

A Brief Analysis[1]

Stephen M. Rosoff, Henry N. Pontell and Robert Tillman's *Profit without Honor: White-Collar Crime and the Looting of America* examines and analyzes the forms, causes and consequences of white-collar crimes (that is, crimes committed mainly by middle- and upper-class individuals in the course of their occupation). The work challenges the popular notion that white-collar crime is not dangerous, and illustrates the prevalence of white-collar crime in business, the government, the medical profession and religious organizations. It shows that white-collar crime has a long and intense history in American society.[2]

Rosoff, Pontell and Tillman stress that the consequences of white-collar crimes are in many ways more damaging than those of street crimes. These consequences fall into three categories: 1) environmental and human cost, 2) economic cost and 3) social cost.[3]

Profit without Honor points out that certain white-collar crimes cause environmental damage, personal injury, sickness and death. The book looks at the harmful effects of the tons of lethal chemicals and toxic waste that are dumped illegally by corporations in the United States. It also examines the dangerous working conditions maintained by U.S. employers in violation of prevailing safety standards. Furthermore, the text indicates that unsafe products made by corporations and sold to consumers result in 30,000 deaths and 20,000,000 injuries a year in America.[4]

Rosoff, Pontell and Tillman show that white-collar crimes cause more financial injury than street crime. They write that the monetary damage from certain white-collar offenses (bribery, fraud, kickbacks, payoffs, computer crimes, consumer fraud, illegal competition, deceptive practices, embezzlement, pilferage, receiving stolen property and securities theft) is estimated to be 250 billion dollars a year, whereas the monetary expense to all victims of personal crimes (robbery, assault, larceny) and household crimes (burglary, motor vehicle theft) is estimated to be 20 billion dollars a year. [5]

Profit without Honor points out that the social cost of white-collar crime (institutional corruption) involves an erosion of trust that Americans place in big business, the government, the medical profession and religious organizations. The book demonstrates that such a lack of trust by the public due to institutional corruption encourages and promotes other types of crimes. It declares that "the existence of elite lawbreaking promotes disrespect for potential street criminals seeking to justify their misconduct."[6] Moreover, the text states that "corrupt banks are central to the operations of international cartels that import billions of dollars in cocaine and other drugs into the United States."[7]

Rosoff, Pontell and Tillman present a number of suggestions for controlling white-collar crime. First, the authors propose new laws that impose tougher penalties on white-collar offenders. Second, they suggest that a system of regulatory codes and administrative agencies need to be created to monitor corporate conduct and respond to criminal violations. Third, the authors stress the necessity to develop internationally agreed upon standards of conduct. Fourth, they point out that the American public has to show less tolerance to those convicted of white-collar crime. [8]

Overall, Rosoff, Pontell and Tillman's work *Profit without Honor: White-Collar Crime and the Looting of America* exemplifies a peacemaking approach to criminology by setting the record straight on the damaging effects of white-collar crime.

NOTES

1. Originally published as Louis Gesualdi, "Rosoff, Pontell and Tillman's *Profit without Honor: White-Collar Crime and Looting in America, " Crime, Law and Social Change 29,* no. 4 (1998): 311-313.

2. Stephen M. Rosoff, Henry N. Pontell, and Robert Tillman, *Profit without Honor: White-Collar Crime and the Looting of America*, Prentice Hall, Inc., 1998.

3. Ibid.

4. Ibid.

5. Ibid.

6. Ibid., p. 414.

7. Rosoff, Pontell, and Tillman's *Profit without Honor: White-Collar: Crime and the Looting of America*, 1998, p. 415.

8. Ibid.

Chapter Fifteen

Tillman's *Broken Promises*

A Brief Examination[1]

Robert Tillman's *Broken Promises: Fraud by Small Business Health Insurers* exemplifies a peacemaking approach to criminology through his examination and analysis of the white collar crimes (scams) that occur in the small group health insurance industry. This industry supplies health insurance to self-employed persons and the employees of small enterprises. His book explains how small group health insurance businesses are vulnerable to fraud and mistreatment.[2]

Tillman describes the most common forms of health insurance fraud: scams involving multiple employer welfare arrangements, employee leasing schemes, bogus labor unions, twenty-four hour plans, and coverage offered by suspicious religious organizations. The author gives many examples on how con artists carry out these scams.[3]

Broken Promises notes that fraudulent small group health insurance businesses victimize many people (usually on the lower end of the socioeconomic ladder). These victimized persons, as a result of these fraudulent businesses, are left with costly medical expenses and no health care coverage. Moreover, Tillman's work makes clear that in numerous cases white collar crimes in health insurance can be viewed as violent crimes. His book illustrates the many individuals who have suffered physical harm, including death, as an outcome of their victimization by white collar criminals in the small group health insurance industry.[4]

Tillman describes two major changes that had serious consequences for the health industry. These two changes involved the withdrawal of most of the large established insurance corporations from the health care market and the passing of the Employee Retirement Income Security Act (ERISA) by

Congress in 1974. The author shows how this withdrawal and the passing of ERISA produced a situation where the need for health benefits among small business employees was strong and the supply of health benefits in legal businesses was extremely low. He points out that in such a situation white collar criminals were able to prosper by creating an illegal market in health insurance.[5]

Broken Promises makes the following suggestions on how to effectively reduce the large amounts of health insurance scams in the United States. First, the book indicates that the laws in respect to ERISA need to be changed. Second, it mentions that adequate health care, possibly through some form of government intervention, needs to be provided to all Americans.[6]

Overall, Robert Tillman's work *Broken Promises: Fraud by Small Business Health Insurers* exemplifies peacemaking criminology by demonstrating the serious harm many people experience as a result of fraudulent small group health insurance businesses.

NOTES

1. Originally published as Louis Gesualdi, "Tillman's *Broken Promises:* A Review," *Crime, Law and Social Change* 31, no. 2 (1999): 151-152.
2. Robert Tillman, *Broken Promises: Fraud by Small Business Health Insurers* (Boston: Northeastern University, 1998).
3. Ibid.
4. Ibid.
5. Ibid.
6. Ibid.

Chapter Sixteen

An Examination of Simon's
Elite Deviance[1]

David R. Simon's *Elite Deviance* examines the harmful acts committed by elites (i.e., persons from the highest levels of society—members of the upper and upper-middle classes). Such acts of great harm include crime against consumers, environmental crime, governmental crimes and corruption of public officials. This book presents an account of the circumstances in which these harmful acts take place.[2]

Simon reveals that the deviant acts of members of the upper and upper-middle classes are not random events. He indicates that such deviance has some of the following essential attributes: (a) it happens because it furthers the continuance of increase of profit and/or power, (b) it is performed with the support of the elites who are in charge of the economic and political organizations, and (c) it may be carried out by elites and/or employees acting on their own behalf.[3]

Elite Deviance examines an institutionalized set of deviant practices by elites from all over the world. The book points out these persons' collaboration with global crime syndicates involved in the $850 billion global narcotics trade and the vast amount of money laundered by legitimate financial institutes, lawyers and other elite professionals.[4]

Simon discusses the present-day characteristics of corporate crime that include antitrust laws, advertising law, and pollution law violations. The author reveals that corporate crime costs American consumers an estimated $261 billion a year, and hundreds of thousands of lives are taken by corporate crime. He indicates that corporate crime is one of the world's most serious social problems.[5]

Elite Deviance explains that in a market economy, "Private businesses make decisions based on making profit" and, as a result, place "the environment in jeopardy."[6] Moreover, the book makes it clear that "pollution is a direct consequence of an economic system in which the profit motive supersedes the concern for the environment."[7]

Simon examines international arms smuggling and global dumping of toxic wastes by big businesses. The author also investigates human rights violations by governments in other countries receiving U.S. foreign and military aid.[8]

Elite Deviance discusses crimes perpetuated by the U.S. government against the people. The book catalogues the secrecy and deception used by government officials to manipulate public opinion and the abuse of power by government officials and agencies. It also examines police brutality and the use of citizens as unwilling guinea pigs by the American government. Simon's text also investigates crimes by governments from different countries on a global level (such as clandestine intervention and war crimes).[9]

The author points out that harmful acts committed by persons from the upper and upper-middle classes hold many negative consequences for society. These consequences include high prices, dangerous products, and the increased motivation to commit harmful acts on the part of the working and lower classes.

Overall, Simon's book *Elite Deviance* exemplifies a peacemaking viewpoint to criminology by its comprehensive treatment on the subject of harmful acts committed by elites.

The main theme of this book is that the source of elite deviance is the structure of society. This work suggests that the market economy must be changed so that people rather than profits are supreme. It proposes a development of economic democracy (i.e., the direct control and management of the businesses and social services by the workers through democratic means).[10]

NOTES

1. Originally published as Louis Gesualdi, "Simon's *Elite Deviance*: A Review," *Journal of Contemporary Criminal Justice* 18, no. 1 (2002): 108-109.

2. David R. Simon, *Elite Deviance* (Boston: Allyn & Bacon, 1999).

3. Ibid.

4. Ibid.

5. Ibid.

6. Ibid., p. 155.

7. Simon, *Elite Deviance,* 1999, p. 157.

8. Ibid.

9. Ibid.

10. Ibid.

Chapter Seventeen

A Review of Coleman's
The Criminal Elite[1]

James William Coleman's *The Criminal Elite: Understanding White-Collar Crime* challenges the popular notion that white-collar crime causes less damage to the American public than street crime. In fact, his book shows that white-collar crime is one of the most serious problems facing the United States today. Coleman's work presents to the reader definitions, types and causes of white-collar crime.[2]

Coleman examines several definitions of white-collar crime given by different social scientists. The author, based on his examination, supports criminologists using the 1996 National White-Collar Crime Center Conference's definition of white-collar crime. The 1996 Conference defines white collar crimes as "illegal or unethical acts that violate fiduciary responsibility of public trust committed by an individual or organization, usually during the course of legitimate occupational activity, by persons of high or respectable social status for personal or organizational gain."[3] Unlike past definitions, Coleman argues the Conference's definition is broader because 1) white-collar crime is no longer restricted to individuals of high societal positions and 2) other related violations of laws such as tax evasion can now be noted as white-collar offenses.[4]

The Criminal Elite discusses the following types of white-collar crime: ripping off the company, fraud and deception, conflicts of interest, bribery and corruption, manipulating the marketplace, violating civil liberties and violent white-collar crimes. Ripping off the company involves employee theft, individual embezzlement, computer crimes and collective embezzlement. Fraud and deception encompass false advertising, consumer fraud, fraud in the professions, financial fraud and tax evasion. Conflicts of interest deal specifically with conflicts of interest in government and the professions.

55

Bribery and corruption include commercial bribery, corruption in criminal justice, and political bribery and corruption. Manipulating the marketplace constitutes unfair business practices, conspiracies and collusion in the professions. Violations of civil liberties consist of discrimination and sexual harassment, violations of privacy, and political harassment and repression. Violent white-collar crimes involve political violence, unsafe workplaces, environmental crimes and unsafe products.[5]

Coleman, in his study, shows that white-collar crime is brought about by the coincidence of three necessary factors. First, there must be motivation for an individual to turn to white collar crime. This motivation is the desire for financial gain, the wish to be seen as successful by others, or the concern of losing what one has. The author argues "the political economy of industrial society, with its enormous surplus and reliance on a system of market exchange, has given rise to a culture of competition that fosters these motivations."[6] The second requirement is the neutralization of moral restrictions that inhibit criminal behavior. On the individual level, this includes the application of numerous rationalizations that excuse the offender's conduct. In the case of organizational crime, large organizations develop the definitions that direct the behavior of their employees. Therefore, criminal actions may be interpreted in such a manner as to make them seem conventional, an unproblematic course of action, or as a required duty of business.[7] Third, there must be opportunity. The author points out throughout his study the abundance of opportunities for white-collar offenders.[8]

The Criminal Elite gives many examples of respected men and women employing the most unethical methods to increase already abundant wealth, of large corporations' lack of concern to the injuries and deaths they caused innocent people, of the government's infractions of human rights, and of the deficiency and corruption of law enforcement. The work, in exemplifying peacemaking criminology, concludes that the "kinds of changes necessary to provide a permanent solution will require a major restructuring of our social and economic relationships."[9]

NOTES

1. Originally published as Louis Gesualdi, "Coleman's *The Criminal Elite: Understanding White-Collar Crime:* A Review," *Sociological Viewpoints* 16, (2000): 65-66.
2. James William Coleman, *The Criminal Elite: Understanding White-Collar Crime* (New York: St. Martin's Press, 1998).
3. Ibid.
4. Ibid., 7-8.
5. Ibid.
6. Ibid., 212.
7. Ibid.
8. Ibid.
9. Ibid., 236.

Chapter Eighteen

Exploitation of Third World Labor

Since the 1980s, most factories and plants that were in the United States have moved to Third World countries. A peacemaking approach to criminology examines the unethical behavior and harmful acts of expanding corporations moving their factories and plants to Third World countries. B. Ehrenreich and A. Fuentes' work, "Life on the global Assembly Line," and A. Foek's study, "Sweatshop Barbie: Exploitation of Third World Labor," provide data that demonstrate the unethical behavior and harmful acts of these expanding corporations.

Ehrenreich and Fuentes' work discusses the life of females in the global economy (expansion of capitalism). Their research indicates the following information:

* Third World females have turned out to be a significant part in the global economy and a major resource for increasing multinational corporations.
* The enormous bulk of low-skilled assembly jobs that go to the Third World are done by females.
* Multinational corporations have a preference for females for assembly line work because they can be legally paid less than males in many countries.
* The U. S. Government is indirectly involved in the low salaries for Third World female workers. It sets the stage by helping countries become low wage shelters for multinational corporations by supporting Third World governments that are capitalist, politically despotic, and not striving for economic autonomy. [1]

Ehrenreich and Fuentes describe the following work conditions of Third World females.

- A majority of Third World factory women perform their work under punishing and hazardous conditions for subsistence level wages or less.
- Work sent abroad to the Third World is often hazardous and usually goes to countries that promise no interference from health and safety policies.
- Electronics assembly makes use of several toxic materials and frequently leads to severe eye problems.
- Situations in the garment and textile industries equal those of 19th century sweatshops.
- Stress is a foremost health risk in all the exported industries.
- High turnover is promoted to keep from paying higher wages to experienced workers, so females are likely to be fired by the age of 23 or 24.[2]

Ehrenreich and Fuentes conclude that Third World females who work in the factories of multinational corporations are exploited to such a degree that the disadvantages to them outweigh the advantage of having a job.[3]

Anton Foek in his work "Sweatshop Barbie: Exploitation of Third World Labor" provides support for Ehrenreich and Fuentes' work by pointing out the following consequences of working in factories like those in Thailand that make Barbie dolls.

- Barbie dolls are made by women and children factory workers in Thailand. These workers are underpaid and overworked. Many suffer illness and death because of their working circumstances.
- These workers have no vacations, no sick days, no union, and no rights. If they become ill, they may just be laid from their job.
- In a Bangkok factory, many of the female workers develop respiratory illnesses from breathing in fabric dust and chemicals. More than ¾ have breathing troubles.
- Other health difficulties of the Thai women and children factory workers involve pains in the neck, hand, and shoulders, nausea, dizziness, memory and hair loss, and sleep disorders.[4]

Foek presents the following reasons why women and children who work in Third World factories and plants will not quit their jobs.

- A majority of the Thai women and children factory workers are from extremely poor areas in northeastern Thailand.
- In these deprived areas, some parents sell their daughters into sex slavery or as cheap labor. Those who are not sold are sent to factories in other parts of Thailand so that they can send some of their scant pay back home to give support to the rest of the family.

- Even in the face of incapacitating illness or death, the Thai women and children factory workers are fearful of leaving their jobs. A woman who loses her job may be dishonored by her family. [5]

Anton Foek indicates that many Third World women and children, such as the Thai workers in Barbie factories, are caught between the destructiveness of poverty and the damaging costs of factory work. The author points out that those who stay working in the factory are likely to suffer for it with devastating sickness and premature death. [6]

If the market economy is unable to end the exploitation and oppression of the workers in Third World nations (as discussed in this chapter), peacemaking criminology, in agreement with David R. Simon (see Chapter 16), proposes a development of a global economic democracy to deal with the exploitation of Third World labor. Economic democracy is the direct control and management of the businesses and social services by the workers through democratic means (see Chapter 22).

NOTES

1. Barbara Ehrenreich and Anette Fuentes, "Life on the Global Assembly Line," *Ms. Magazine,* January 1981.

2. Ibid.

3. Ibid.

4. Anton Foek, "Sweatshop Barbie: Exploitation of Third World Labor," *The Humanist,* January/February 1997.

5. Ibid.

6. Ibid.

Chapter Nineteen

The Work of John Augustus

Peacemaking Criminology[1]

The United States has one of the largest and most costly prison systems in the world, as it incarcerates more of its population than most nations.[2] In response to this state of affairs peacemaking criminology has developed as a branch of criminology to champion alternatives to incarceration. Peacemaking criminology involves not an authoritarian but a humane, nonviolent and scientific approach in its treatment of crime and the offender.[3] It looks at crime as just one of the many types of suffering that illustrate human existence. Efforts to prevent such suffering, according to peacemaking criminologists, should include a major reconstruction of America's social institutions, such as the economic system and the criminal justice system, so that they no longer produce suffering.[4] Unemployment and incarceration are, respectively, aspects of America's economic system and criminal justice system that need alterations. In brief, the U.S., as a society pays no heed to prevention but rather follows the belief of imprisonment and punishment. Peacemaking criminology seeks prevention and rehabilitation to pursue the principles of social justice and human rights.[5]

The precepts of peacemaking criminology can be traced back to John Augustus who in 1841 introduced probation to the criminal justice system in the United States. His development of probation, like peacemaking criminology, was based on a humane, non authoritarian, and a scientific approach to deal with the offender. Augustus' view was that the "object of the law is to reform criminals, and to prevent crime and not to punish maliciously, or from a spirit of revenge."[6]

From 1841 to 1858, John Augustus had bailed out from jail 1150 males and 794 females. Of the two thousand people he bailed, only 10 proved ungrateful or absconded. In addition to those he bailed, he had helped over three thousand females who were destitute. Overall, he worked with offenders categorized as drunkards, extremely poor, unemployed, prostitutes and for the benefit of juveniles. [7]

Augustus performed many duties for the people who were placed on probation under his care. He made sure the person attended school or engaged in honest employment. He often arranged living accommodations and maintained records of all the cases he handled. In some cases, Augustus had some of his clients living in his own home. This sometimes involved rehabilitation of the offender with a drinking problem or providing shelter for women and children who were poor, unemployed and had no place to go. [8]

John Augustus insisted that the offenders who were drunkards had to "take the pledge" or promise not to drink liquor. Over 80% of the drunkards that he worked with became temperate and orderly citizens and gained employment. He showed that drunkards on probation under his care had greater success of rehabilitation than the punitive methods of jail or house corrections. For instance, he noted that the largest numbers of people in jail in the county of Suffolk in 1841-42 were drunkards. Augustus indicated that almost all the drunkards "were sentenced more than once, some as many as fifteen or twenty times" and that frequently only a few days would pass between the release and return of offenders to jail as a result of continued drunkenness. Augustus showed conclusively that imprisonment as a punitive measure, and in the extreme, "had a very slight tendency to produce the reformation of those who are its subjects."[9] In other words, jail or extreme punishment in general does not reform drunkards, that is, individuals with a substance abuse problem.

John Augustus' work representing peacemaking criminology in action had helped reduce crime without incarceration. His labors, as stated previously, were humane and non-authoritarian (that is, providing a home, working to rehab the drunkard, helping to gain employment for the person) and scientific (that is, keeping records of observations and applying methods that were found to be successful). Furthermore, similar to peacemaking criminology, he promoted alternative sanctions rather than prison in dealing with certain offenders.

Augustus' work can provide a basis for the development and further growth of peacemaking criminology. In examining American prisons, there are similarities with the kinds of people who are incarcerated today and the kinds of individuals John Augustus was able to rehabilitate outside of prison.

There is a telltale pattern to the person incarcerated today in the United States. Thirty-five percent were unemployed at the time of their arrest and most of those who had been working had very low paying jobs. Drug offenders represent the largest proportionate growth of inmates, increasing from an estimated 58,000 in 1983 to 354,000 in 1993. Of all state prisoners 62% were convicted of nonviolent crimes, and of all federal prisoners 75% were in for nonviolent crimes.[10] John Augustus' clients also were mostly poor, unemployed, drunkards, that is, had a substance abuse problem and were mostly nonviolent. Based on the types of people that are in prison and in light of the success of John Augustus' work, alternative sanctions would be more effective in dealing with most of today's prison population. Peacemaking criminologists would and do support alternatives to incarceration. Alternative sanctions such as halfway houses, drug rehabilitation outside of prison, community service and civic restitution are similar to the kinds of methods that Augustus applied to his clients.

Many studies examine alternatives to incarceration, albeit in the few cases in the United States where alternatives are used, and present the following findings: Alternatives to incarceration 1) are cheaper than prison; 2) have lower rates of recidivism than incarceration; 3) are tougher, more demanding and more rigorous than having nonviolent offenders sitting around in prisons and learning lessons from dangerous violent inmates; and 4) relieve overcrowding and provide more room to put away dangerous offenders who need to be separated from society.[11] Moreover, research indicates that drug rehabilitation, community service work, civic restitution and halfway houses would increase public safety.[12] The research clearly demonstrates the failure of today's prisons, as well as during John Augustus' time, in dealing with many types of crime (in particular, people with drug or alcohol problems), and this research indicates the effectiveness of alternative sanctions in cases involving nonviolent crimes.[13]

Considering that most prisoners in America are convicted of nonviolent crimes and were unemployed and/or poor at the time of their arrest, a full time employment bill would logically prevent many types of crimes. Today, by comparison, Scandinavian countries as well as Japan and Holland have low unemployment rates (close to 0% unemployment) and have very low crime rates and very low imprisonment rates.[14] Part of John Augustus' success was that he found employment for many of his clients. The employment of his clients played a role in the success of their rehabilitation.[15] Peacemaking criminologists, expanding on Augustus' work and in their efforts to prevent suffering, would support the implementation of a full employment bill, a nonviolent, non-authoritarian and humane way to prevent crime.

America's prison system, as one of the world's largest and most costly prison systems, contains 1.2 million people at a cost of over 30 billion dollars a year.[16] Research indicates the ineffectiveness of incarceration by showing there is no association between spending money to incarcerate more people and a lower crime rate.[17] For instance, even though the U. S. maintains such a high imprisonment rate, America still has the highest crime rate among industrialized nations.[18] A peacemaking criminological approach is needed to cut the crime rate in the United States. As we have seen, John Augustus' work was quite successful and exemplified the principles of peacemaking criminology. The implementation of alternative sanctions and a full employment bill is a continuation and expansion of John Augustus' successful work and would be supported by peacemaking criminology. In conclusion, based on the data presented in this chapter, the crime and recidivism rates in America would decline as an outcome of the development and growth of a peacemaking criminological viewpoint.

NOTES

1. Originally published as Louis Gesualdi, "The Work of John Augustus: Peacemaking Criminology," *Academy of Criminal Justice Sciences ACJS Today* 17, no. 3 (1999): 1, 3-4.
2. Victor Kappeler, Mark Blumberg, Gary Potter, *The Mythology of Crime and Criminal Justice* (Illinois: Waveland Press, 1996).
3. John R. Fuller, *Criminal Justice: A Peacemaking Perspective* (Boston: Allyn and Bacon, 1998).
4. Harold E. Pepinsky and Richard Quinney, eds., *Criminology as Peacemaking*, (Bloomington: Indiana University Press, 1991).
5. Fuller, *Criminal Justice: A Peacemaking Perspective.*
6. John Augustus, *John Augustus: First Probation Officer* (New Jersey: Patterson Smith, 1972).
7. Ibid, 1-23.
8. Ibid, 23.
9. Ibid, 31.
10. . Peter T. Elikann, *The Tough on Crime Myth* (New York: Insight Books, 1996).
11. Ibid.
12. Ibid.
13. Ibid.
14. Ibid, 32-34.
15. Augustus, *John Augustus: First Probation Officer,* 1972.
16. Elikann, *The Tough on Crime Myth,* 47-49.
17. Ibid.
18. Kappeler, Blumberg, and Potter, *The Mythology of Crime and Criminal Justice,* 1996.

Chapter Twenty

The Popular Notion about Teenage Violence[1]

Mike Males' *The Scapegoat Generation: America ' s War on Adolescents* challenges the popular notion about America's teenagers being inherently violent. It notes that the media, certain law enforcement experts and many government officials manipulate information to scapegoat teenagers for America's high rates of violent crime and drug deaths. His work presents data that show violent crime among youth is founded in social conditions such as poverty and income disparity and not age demographics and race.[2]

Males examines and analyzes data including the World Health Statistics Annual (1994), Bureau of Justice Statistics, U.S. Census Bureau, and California Center for Health Statistics and does not find support for the popular claim that violence is innate to teenagers. The author indicates that in 1993 the FBI reported that 70% of the murderers of children/youth were adults— not other youth. He also notes that in 1993, 92 percent of the slayers of adults were adults. Moreover, the author points out that within families, parents are six times more likely to murder their teenager than the other way around.[3]

The Scapegoat Generation shows that America's teenagers account for only 2% of drug deaths. These rates are far lower than the rates found among adults. The book demonstrates that the biggest drug danger the United States faces is the high rates of hard drug abuse, and injury and death among middle aged adults.[4]

Mike Males indicates that violent youth crime in America is due to youth poverty. The author notes that teenagers, regardless of race, are not more violent than adults. He points out that if one adjusts the racial crime rate for the number of individuals living in extreme poverty, non-whites have a crime rate similar to that of whites at every age level. Furthermore, Males explains that American social policies force 25% of our youth to grow up in poverty, leading to high rates of violence not found in other Western nations. Specifically, America raises three to eight times more children in poverty than other Western nations.[5]

The Scapegoat Generation shows that the United States, unlike other Western nations, does not spend money to reduce poverty. It points out that America's focus is on more police, increased building of prisons, and longer prison sentences imposed at younger ages. The book demonstrates that there is no association between money spent to incarcerate and a reduced rate of crime among teenagers and adults.[6]

Overall, Males' work *The Scapegoat Generation: America ' s War on Adolescent* supports a peacemaking approach to criminology by indicating that America's focus on more police, increased building of prisons, and longer prison sentences imposed on younger ages (part of retributive justice) does not reduce the rate of crime among teenagers and adults. His work sets the record straight on how the media, many government officials and certain law enforcement experts unfairly scapegoat adolescents for America's problems.

NOTES

1. Originally published as Louis Gesualdi, "Males' *The Scapegoat Generation: America ' s War on Adolescents*: A Review," *Sociological Viewpoints 15,* (1999): 67.
2. Mike Males, *The Scapegoat Generation: America ' s War on Adolescents* (Maine: Common Courage Press, 1996).
3. Ibid.
4. Ibid.
5. Ibid.
6. Ibid.

Chapter Twenty-One

Peacemaking Acts and Programs to Cut Adult and Teen Crime[1]

There is a pattern to the persons incarcerated in the United States. Thirty-five percent were unemployed at the time of their arrest and most of those who had been working had very low-paying jobs. Drug offenders represent the largest proportional growth of inmates increasing from 8% of the prison population in the early 1980s to approximately 25% in the late 1990s. Of all state prisoners, 62% were convicted of nonviolent crimes, and of all federal prisoners, 75% were in for nonviolent crimes. [2]

America presently maintains, among the world's democratic nations, the largest and most expensive prison system, with approximately 1.5 million people at a cost of over 30 billion dollars a year. For every 100,000 people in the U.S., 600 were behind bars in 1997. By way of comparison, Great Britain incarcerated 100 out of 100,000; Italy, 85; Japan, 37; and Holland, 65. [3] Moreover, the federal prison system in America was operating at 46 percent over capacity and state prisons were 31 percent over capacity. [4] Research indicates the ineffectiveness of incarceration by showing there is no association between money spent to incarcerate and a reduced rate of crime among adults and teenagers. [5] For instance, even though the U.S. maintains the highest imprisonment rate among the world's democratic nations, America still has the highest adult and teen crime rate among these nations. [6]

The purpose of this chapter is to present political acts and programs from a peacemaking approach to criminology that may very well reverse this situation. A peacemaking perspective to criminology, as stated previously, is a humanistic approach to criminology. This approach views crime as just one of the many forms of suffering (such as war, poverty, unemployment and others) that characterize human existence. It is involved with the advancement of humane, non violent, non-authoritarian and scientific ways to reduce (and eventually end) suffering and oppression. A peacemaking viewpoint proposes major changes in the social and economic structures in the United States so that they no longer bring about suffering and oppression. [7]

A peacemaking approach to criminology would, I argue, campaign for and support the following political acts and programs: 1) a full employment bill, 2) a real minimum wage, 3) a nationalized health care bill, 4) a bill ending the prohibition of drugs, and 5) the implementation of intermediate sanctions. The adult and teen crime rates as well as recidivism rates in America would probably decline significantly as an outcome of these acts and programs.

First, since most prisoners in America were convicted of nonviolent crimes, were unemployed and/or poor at the time of their arrest, a full time employment bill and a real minimum wage (that is, a salary that would provide a good standard of living) would logically, and in a humane way, prevent many types of crimes. Other countries, unlike the U.S., (such as the Scandinavian countries, Japan, Holland) that have low unemployment rates (close to 0% unemployment) and a good standard of living (this includes good housing, health care and educational opportunities for the population at large) have very low crime rates and very low imprisonment rates. [8]

Violent youth crime and adult crime in America are due to poverty. American social policies force 25% of our youth to grow up in poverty leading to high rates of violence not found in other Western nations. Specifically, America raises three to eight times more children in poverty than other Western nations. [9]

A full time employment bill and a real minimum wage would provide poor adults and poor teens with a real chance to better their lives. In fact, such a bill and wage would not only be beneficial to the poor but probably to almost all Americans.

Second, ending the prohibition of drugs and a nationalized health care bill are needed in dealing with the drug problem in the U.S. The reasoning behind this argument is that drug decriminalization and nationalized health care became public policy in Holland, and drug use dropped considerably in that country. Specifically, the consumption of marijuana in the Netherlands has decreased from 10 percent of the population in 1976 to around 3 percent in the 1990s. The percentage of people using marijuana in Holland is considerably less than in the United States where marijuana possession is still illegal. [10] Also, in the Netherlands, decriminalized cocaine is used by 1200 percent fewer people than in the United States. [11] Drug use dropped significantly in Holland because of educational and rehabilitation programs that are part of nationalized health care. Law enforcement did not play a role in this very significant decline of drug use.

America's drug strategy, on the other hand, which is based on law enforcement (that is, the war on drugs), has only been effective in increasing the numbers of arrests, convictions and imprisonment. It has failed in reducing drug abuse and addiction.[12] Recent research presents the following facts: 1) Presently, cocaine is inexpensive and more abundant than ever, 2) emergency room visits are high across the U.S. for adverse reactions to drugs, 3) teen drug use is very high, and 4) the number of people most in need of drug treatment is large.[13]

The problem with America's current drug strategy "lies with spending most of the money on law enforcement and interdiction (supply) and too small an amount on rehabilitation and preventive education (demand)." [14] For instance, although the United States "spends more than 50 million dollars a year on research to prevent crime, 15 billion dollars is spent annually on drug enforcement."[15]

Research shows that "treatment is more effective in cutting drug use than law enforcement."[16] For instance, a 1997 study by RAND's Drug Policy Research Center concluded that treatment (rehabilitation) is the most effective tool in the fight against drug abuse, finding that rehabilitation reduces 15 times more serious crime than mandatory minimum sentences. Moreover, several studies sponsored by the National Institute on Drug Abuse have shown that drug rehabilitation programs on the whole are successful in reducing the levels of drug abuse and crime among participants (adults and teens) and in increasing their ability to hold a job. Furthermore, drug treatment costs less than imprisonment. For instance, in New York State the cost of most drug-free outpatient care runs about $2,700 - $3,600 per person per year, and the cost of residential drug treatment is $17,000-$20,000 per participant per year.[17] These expenses are way less than keeping an inmate in a New York State prison at an approximate cost of $30,000 a year.[18]

Overall, studies indicate that drug laws make the drug problems among adults and teens in the United States worse. There are also other benefits to be derived by ending the prohibition of drugs. Repealing drug laws will save at least 17 billion dollars a year in law enforcement, and organized crime groups would be dealt a severe setback.[19] Therefore, Americans need to view the drug problem as more of a public health issue than a criminal justice system problem.[20]

Third, prisons are mainly needed to separate dangerous violent offenders from society in order to rehabilitate them and not as a primary form of correction. Intermediate sanctions or alternatives to incarceration are more humane and effective ways to deal with nonviolent adult and teen offenders. These alternatives include community service, drug rehabilitation outside prison, halfway houses and civic restitution.

Many studies examine alternatives to incarceration and present the following findings: 1) Alternatives to incarceration are cheaper than prison; 2) they have lower rates of recidivism than incarceration; 3) intermediate sanctions are tougher, more demanding and more rigorous than having nonviolent adult and teen offenders sitting around in prisons and learning lessons from dangerous violent inmates; 4) they relieve overcrowding and provide more room to put away dangerous offenders who need to be separated from society.[21] Moreover, research indicates that drug rehabilitation (as part of nationalized health care), community service work, civic restitution and halfway houses would increase public safety. The research demonstrates the failure of the incarceration of offenders in dealing with offenses (in particular, nonviolent offenses) and clearly describes the effectiveness of alternatives to prison for nonviolent offenses in general.[22]

The criminal justice system in the United States has developed and enforced unnecessary laws (drug laws), harsh punishment (nonviolent offenders in prison), and has misplaced social resources (money spent to imprison people). It has failed to deal with many societal problems and adult and teen offenders in the United States.

In conclusion, a peacemaking approach to criminology could not only support the implementation of different intermediate sanctions but also changes in the social and economic structures of American society. These changes, as stated previously, would include a full employment bill, a real minimum wage, nationalized health care and ending the prohibition of drugs. Such political acts and programs would provide adult and teen offenders rehabilitation and a real chance to better their lives.

NOTES

1. Originally published as Louis Gesualdi, "Peacemaking Acts and Programs to Cut Adult and Teen Crime," *Sociological Viewpoints* 19, (2003): 7-10.

2. Victor Kappeler, Mark Blumberg, and Gary Potter, *The Mythology of Crime and Criminal Justice* (Illinois, Waveland Press, 2000): 158 and Elikann, *The Tough on Crime Myth* (New York: Insight Books, 1996): 50-51, 162.

3. Kappeler, Blumberg and Potter, *The Mythology of Crime and Criminal Justice,* 259 and Elikann, *The Tough on Crime Myth,* 32, 47-49.

4. Elikann, *The Tough on Crime Myth,* 44 and Bureau of Justice Statistics, U.S. Department of Justice, "Jail Inmates, 1993-1994," April, 1995.

5. Mike Males, *Framing Youth: Ten Myths About the Next Generation* (Maine: Common Courage Press, 1999), and *The Scapegoat Generation: America's War on Adolescent* (Maine: Common Courage Press, 1996), and Elikann, *The Tough on Crime Myth ,* 127-145.

6. See Kappeler, Blumberg and Potter, *The Mythology of Crime and Criminal Justice,* Males, *Framing Youth,* and *The Scapegoat Generation,* and Steven F. Messner and Richard Rosenfeld, *Crime and the American Dream* (California: Wadsworth Inc., 1994).

7. Harold Pepinsky and Richard Quinney, eds., *Criminology as Peacemaking* (Bloomington: Indiana University Press, 1991).

8. Elikann, *The Tough on Crime Myth,* 32-44.

9. Males, *The Scapegoat Generation.*

10. Kappeler, Blumberg and Potter, *The Mythology of Crime and Criminal Justice,* Jonathan Blank, *Sex, Drugs and Democracy,* Film Documentary, 1994, Netherlands: Red Hat Productions (DVD), 2001, and Arnold Trebach and Eddy Engelman, "Why Not Decriminalize?," *New Perspective Quarterly,* 1989.

11. Trebach and Engelman, "Why Not Decriminalize?"

12. See Elikann, *The Tough on Crime Myth*, 163.

13. Ibid., 163-164.

14. Ibid., 168-169.

15. Ibid., 15.

16. Elikann, *The Tough on Crime Myth*, 13, and Correctional Association of New York, New York, NY, 1998.

17. *Correctional Association of New York,* New York, NY, 1998.

18. Ibid.

19. Kappeler, Blumberg, and Potter, *The Mythology of Crime and Criminal Justice,* 171-172 and Ethan A. Nadelmann, "Drug Prohibition in the United States: Costs, Consequences, and Alternatives," *Science* 245, no. 4921 (1989).

20. Kappeler, Blumberg and Potter, *The Mythology of Crime and Criminal Justice*, 143-172.

21. Elikann, *The Tough on Crime Myth*, 14.

22. Kappeler, Blumberg and Potter, *The Mythology of Crime and Criminal Justice*, and Elikann, *The Tough on Crime Myth.*

Chapter Twenty-Two

A Development of
Economic Democracy[1]

There have been many consequences as a result of the global expansion of the market economy over the last thirty years. Positive consequences include tremendous developments in communication, transportation and technology that produce great amounts of goods and services. However, there have been negative consequences because of the expansion of the market economy, including the following:

- The majority of the world's toxic wastes (produced by highly technological developed countries) are dumped in third world countries in an unsafe, hazardous manner.[2]
- Since 1970, the world's forests have declined from 4.4 square miles per 1000 people to 2.8 square miles per 1000.
- A quarter of the world's fish stock has been depleted or is in danger of being depleted and another 44 percent are being fished at their biological limit.[3]
- 36 of the world's 40 poorest countries export food to North America.
- In Africa, half the population suffers from protein deficiencies, and yet, they export protein foods to Europe.[4]
- The average African household today consumes 20 percent less than it did 25 years ago.
- The world's 225 richest individuals, of whom 60 are Americans with total assets of $311 billion, have a combined wealth of over $1 trillion—equal to the annual income of the poorest 47 percent of the entire world's population.[5]
- More and more work is exported to Third World countries because the work is often hazardous. These countries are low wage havens for big

businesses, and they guarantee no interference from health and safety regulations.[6]
• Air, water and land throughout the world are being poisoned due to exported work by big businesses.
• Unemployment and poverty, under a market economy, continue to exist throughout the world bringing hardship to and threatening the lives of hundreds of millions to possibly a few billion people.[7]

Unemployment, underemployment, poverty, unsafe work conditions, unsafe products, destruction of the environment, and other social problems have always been a major result of the market economy for at least 200 years, when it got its start in England.[8]

This chapter presents the initial stages of a plan for a development of economic democracy as discussed by Daniel DeLeon.[9] If the market economy is unable to reverse the above social problems, a peacemaking approach to criminology supports the development of such a system. An economic democratic system may very well reverse the above social problems associated with the market economy.

Economic democracy is the shared ownership or domination by the workers of the factories, mills, mines, railroads, land and all other devices of producing. Economic democracy involves the making of goods to satisfy human being requirements, not, as in the market economy, which involves the making of goods for only selling and profit. Economic democracy means true command and management of the industries and social services by the workers through a democratic government based on their economic organization and not controlled and managed by a fraction of a percentage of the population as in the market economy.[10]

Today workers in their respective countries may have the means and the reasons to develop an economy based on democracy and not on profit (as in the market economy). The means include such technology as computers that enable workers to make contact with each other in very short periods of time in order to develop an economic democratic system. The reasons include ending the destruction of our global environment, unsafe work places, unsafe products, unemployment, underemployment, poverty and other social problems. To develop economic democracy, the workers need to prepare on both the political and economic fields.[11]

To develop economic democracy, political agreement under the emblem of a mass political party of labor is needed. The purpose of the party is to teach workers of the need to do away with the market economy, to crusade for the development of class thinking unions, and to declare the power of the working class at the ballot box. The party must also attempt to seize and take apart the political state----the current territorial kind of government—and thus open the process for a different type of government, a cooperating democracy based on industry. [12]

To develop economic democracy, workers also have to join together as a class by organizing new unions. These democratic, rank and file governed unions, made along the programs of industry, while fighting day to day battles for higher pay and a better work environment, are inspired by a bigger goal: supplanting control of the industries and services by a fraction of a percentage of the population with social possession and democratic workers' domination. [13]

While fighting day to day struggles, these unions would strive at directing the whole working class—employed and unemployed, blue collar and white collar—in all occupations. Through an arrangement of elected and retractable representatives, the various unions would be combined by industry and tied together into a big union which would direct a united encounter against the wealthy few who possess and govern the means of producing and apportioning. When the greater number of workers support economic democracy, this big union would back up the determination made at the ballot box by grabbing, maintaining and handling the industries and services of the land in the social interest. [14]

The unions would then advance the governing parts of an economic democratic society. There would be a truly democratic government in which the workers would be in charge of their own economic safety and welfare. [15]

Under economic democracy, all control will start from the workers integrally united in unions. In each workplace, the workers will elect whatever committees or representatives are needed to facilitate production. Within each workplace, the workers will cooperate immediately in conceiving and setting up all strategies essential for effective procedures. [16]

Besides electing all needed workplace representatives, the workers will also elect representatives to a local and national committee of their occupation—and to a central house of representatives representing all occupations. This central house of representatives will arrange and balance production in all fields of the economy. All people elected to any position in the economic democracy government (the workplace, local committee, national committee or central house of representatives) will be immediately answerable to the workers. They will be subjected to dismissal at any time that a majority of those who elected them determine it is needed. [17]

In conclusion, a development of economic democracy needs great efforts of planning and instructional work. It requires constructing a political party of economic democracy to do away with the market economy and to teach the majority of workers about the necessity for economic democracy. It requires constructing a union uniting all workers in a class-conscious operation and to plan for them to acquire, control and administer the equipment of production. [18]

NOTES

1. Most of this chapter was Louis Gesualdi, "A Development of Economic Democracy" (unpublished paper) originally presented at the Diversity in Research and Society Conference at State University of New York, Farmingdale, NY, April 26, 2001.

2. David Simon, *Elite Deviance* (Boston: Allyn and Bacon, 1999).

3. Kofi Annan, "Astonishing Facts!" *New York Times*, September 4, 1998, Section 4, p. 16.

4. *Oxfam America,* 1985.

5. Annan, "Astonishing Facts!," 16.

6. Simon, *Elite Deviance.*

7. Socialist Labor Party, *Why America Needs Industrial Democracy* (California: Socialist Labor Party, 2000), and Socialist Labor Party, *The Socialist Programs: What If and How It Developed* (California: Socialist Labor Party, 2000), and Simon, *Elite Deviance.*

8. Socialist Labor Party, *Why America Needs Industrial Democracy,* and Socialist Labor Party, *The Socialist Programs.*

9. Daniel DeLeon, *Socialist Reconstruction of Society* (California: New York Labor News, 1977), and Daniel DeLeon, *Socialist Landmarks* (California: New York Labor News, 1952).

10. "The Industrial Democracy of Socialism," *The People*, Vol. 111, no. 3,June 2001, p. 8, Linda Featheringill, "Workers Have to Have a Plan," *The People,* Vol. 106, no. 6, September 1996, "What is Socialism?," *The People,* Vol. 105, no. 6, June 24, 1995, Socialist Labor Party, *Why America Needs Industrial Democracy*, Socialist Labor Party, *The Socialist Programs*, DeLeon, *Socialist Reconstruction of Society,* and DeLeon, *Socialist Landmarks.*

11. Ibid.
12. Ibid.
13. Ibid.
14. Ibid.
15. Ibid.
16. Ibid.
17. Ibid.
18. Ibid.

References

Annan, Kofi. "Astonishing Facts!" *New York Times,* September 4, 1998.

Appelbaum, Richard P., and William J. Chambliss. *Sociology: A Brief Introduction.* New York: Longman, 1997.

———. *Sociology.* New York: HarperCollins, 1995.

Augustus, John. *John Augustus: First Probation Officer.* New Jersey: Patterson Smith, 1972.

Bernstein, B. "Qualifying for Affirmative Action." *New York Newsday,* August 9, 1995.

B. J. S. Bulletin, *Bureau of Justice Statistics Bulletin, Criminal Victimization,* 1993, 1989.

Bohm, Robert M. *Deathquest: An Introduction to Theory and Practice of Capital Punishment in the United States.* Cincinnati: Anderson Publishing Company, 1999.

Braswell, Michael, John Fuller, and Bo Lozoff. *Corrections, Peacemaking and Restorative Justice: Transforming Individuals and Institutions.* Cincinnati, OH: Anderson Publishing Company, 2001.

Bureau of Justice Statistics, U.S. Department of Justice, "Jail Inmates, 1993-1994," April, 1995.

Cocco, Marie. "White Men Deprived? Name a Couple of Dozen?" *New York Newsday,* March 30, 1995.

Coleman, James W. *The Criminal Elite: Understanding White-Collar Crime.* New York: St. Martin's Press, 1998.

Correctional Association of New York, New York, NY, 1998.

DeLeon, Daniel. *Socialist Reconstruction of Society.* California: New York Labor News, 1977.

———. *Socialist Landmarks.* California: New York Labor News, 1952.

Ehrenreich, Barbara, and Fuentes, Annette. "Life on the Global Assembly Line." *Ms. Magazine,* January 1981.

Elikann, Peter. *The Tough on Crime Myth.* New York: Insight Books, 1996.

Eshleman, John R. and Barbara G. Cashion. *Sociology.* Boston: Little, Brown and Company, 1985.

Featheringill, Linda, "Workers Have to Have a Plan," *The People,* Vol. 106, no. 6 (September 1996).

Foek, Anton. "Sweatshop Barbie: Exploitation of Third World Labor." *The Humanist,* January/February 1997.

Fuller, John R. *Criminal Justice: A Peacemaking Perspective.* Boston: Allyn and Bacon, 1998.

Gesualdi, Louis. "Peacemaking Acts and Programs to Cut Adult and Teen Crime." *Sociological Viewpoints* 19, (2003): 7-10.

———. "Simon's *Elite Deviance*: A Review." *Journal of Contemporary Criminal Justice* 18, no. 1 (2002): 108-109.

———. "A Review of Michael Braswell, John Fuller and Bo Lozoff's book *Corrections, Peacemaking and Restorative Justice: Transforming Individuals and Institutions.*" *International Social Science Review* 76, no. 3 & 4 (2001): 141.

———. "A Development of Economic Democracy." Unpublished paper, presented at the Diversity in Research and Society Conference at State University of New York, Farmingdale, NY, April 26, 2001.

———. "Popular Notions of Affirmative Action: A Criticism." *Sociological Viewpoints* 17, (2001): 55-57.

———. "Simon and Hagan's *White-Collar Deviance:* A Review." *Journal of Contemporary Criminal Justice* 16, no. 4 (2000): 457-459.

———. "Kappeler, Blumberg and Potter's *The Mythology of Crime and Criminal Justice, 3*[rd] *Edition:* A Review." *International Social Science Review* 75, no. 3 & 4 (2000): 68-69.

———. "Coleman's *The Criminal Elite: Understanding White-Collar Crime:* A Review." *Sociological Viewpoints* 16, (2000): 65-66.

———. "The Work of John Augustus: Peacemaking Criminology." *Academy of Criminal Justice Sciences ACJS Today* 17, no. 3 (1999): 1, 3-4.

———. "Bohm's *Deathquest: An Introduction to the Theory of Capital Punishment in the United States:* A Review." *Crime, Law and Social Change* 31, no. 2 (1999): 154-155.

———. "Reiman's *The Rich Get Richer and the Poor Get Prison:* A Review." *Crime, Law and Social Change* 31, no. 2 (1999): 152-153.

———. "Rosoff, Pontell and Tillman's *Profit without Honor: White-Collar Crime and Looting in America:* A Review." *Crime, Law and Social Change* 29, no. 4 (1998): 311-313.

———. "Tillman's *Broken Promises:* A Review." *Crime, Law and Social Change* 31, no. 2 (1999): 67.

———. "Males' *The Scapegoat Generation: America 's War on Adolescents*: A Review." *Sociological Viewpoints* 15, (1999): 67.

———. "Van Ness and Heetderks Strong's *Restoring Justice.*" *Journal of Criminal Justice* 15, no. 3 (1999): 354-357.

———. "Don't Blame Mom for Crime." *The Humanist.* May/June 1998.

———. "John R. Fuller's *Criminal Justice: A Peacemaking Perspective.*" *Crime, Law and Social Change* 29, no. 1 (1998): 84.

———. "Walker, Spohn and Delone's *The Color of Justice.*" *Crime, Law and Social Change* 28, no. 4 (1997): 183-184.

———. "Steinberg's *Turning Back:* A Review." *The Humanist* 57, no. 4 (1997):

———. "Kappeler, Blumberg and Potter's *The Mythology of Crime and Criminal Justice, 2*[nd] *Edition:* A Review." *Journal of Contemporary Criminal Justice* 13, no. 4, (1997): 354-357.

———. "Messner and Rosenfeld's *Crime and the American Dream*: A Review." *Crime, Law and Social Change* 26, no. 1 (1997): 96-97.

———. "Williams and Kornblum's *Growing Up Poor*: A Review." *Teaching Sociology* 16, no. 2 (1988): 210.

———. "Steinberg's *Ethnic Myth: Race, Ethnicity and Class.*" *The Journal of Ethnic Studies* 11, no. 4 (1984): 132-134.

Hacker, Andrew. *Two Nations: Black and White, Separate, Hostile, Unequal.* New York: Charles Scribner's Sons, 1992.

Kappeler, Victor, Mark Blumberg, and Gary Potter. *The Mythology of Crime and Criminal Justice.* Illinois: Waveland Press, 2000 and 1996.

Males, Mike. *Framing Youth: Ten Myths About the Next Generation.* Maine: Common Courage Press, 1999.

———. *The Scapegoat Generation: America 's War on Adolescent.* Maine: Common Courage Press, 1996.

Messner, Steven, and Richard Rosenfeld. *Crime and the American Dream.* California: Wadsworth Incorporated, 1994.

Moynihan, Daniel P. "Defining Deviancy Down." *The American Scholar*, Winter 1993.

Nadelmann, Ethan. "Drug Prohibition in the United States: Costs, Consequences, and Alternatives." *Science* 245, no. 4921 (1989): 939-947.

Oxfam America, 1985.

Pepinsky, Harold, and Richard Quinney. eds. *Criminology as Peacemaking.* Bloomington: Indiana University Press, 1991.

Rand, Michael R., James P. Lynch, and David Cantor. "Criminal Victimization, 1973-95." *Bureau of Justice of Statistics, National Crime Victimization Survey,* 1997.

Reiman, Jeffrey. *The Rich Get Richer and the Poor Get Prison: Ideology, Class and Criminal Justice.* Boston: Allyn and Bacon, 1998.

Rosoff, Stephen, Henry N. Pontell, and Robert Tillman. *Profit without Honor: White-Collar Crime and the Looting of America.* Upper Saddle River, NJ: Prentice Hall, Incorporated, 1998.

Sex, Drugs and Democracy. Documentary Film, directed by Jonathan Blank. 1994. Netherlands: Red Hat Productions, 2001. DVD.

Simon, David. *Elite Deviance.* Boston: Allyn and Bacon, 1999.

Simon, David R., and Frank Hagan. *White-Collar Deviance.* Boston: Allyn and Bacon, 1999.

Snyder, Howard N. "Arrests of Youth 1990." *Juvenile Justice Bulletin, U.S. Department of Justice,* January 1992.

Socialist Labor Party. *Why America Needs Industrial Democracy.* California: Socialist Labor Party, 2000.

Socialist Labor Party. *The Socialist Programs: What If and How It Developed.* California: Socialist Labor Party, 2000.

Steinberg, Stephen. *Turning Back: The Retreat from Racial Justice in American Thought and Policy.* Boston: Beacon Press, 1995.

Steinberg, Stephen. *The Ethnic Myth: Race, Ethnicity and Class in America.* Boston: Beacon Press, 1981.

Tillman, Robert. *Broken Promises: Fraud by Small Business Health Insurers.* Boston: Northeastern University, 1998.

"The Industrial Democracy of Socialism," *The People,* Vol. 111, no. 3 (June 2001).

Trebach, Arnold, and Eddy Engelman. "Why Not Decriminalize?" *New Perspective Quarterly.* Summer (1989): 40-45.

U.S. Bureau of the Census, Washington: Government Printing Office, 1993 and 1970.

Van Ness, Daniel, and Karen H. Strong. *Restoring Justice.* Cincinnati, OH: Anderson, 1997.

Walker, Samuel, Cassie Spohn, and Miriam DeLone. *The Color of Justice: Race, Ethnicity, and Crime in America.* California: Wadsworth Publishing, Company, 1996.

"What is Socialism?," *The People,* Vol. 105, no. 6 (June 24, 1995).

Williams, Terry, and William Kornblum. *Growing Up Poor.* Lexington, MA: Lexington Books, 1988.

Wilson, James Q. "What to do about Crime." *Commentary,* September 1994.

Index